2/99
13

Patrick Turnbull

CORSICA

B. T. Batsford Ltd, *London*

First published 1976
© Patrick Turnbull 1976
ISBN 0 7134 3134 2

Typeset by
Input Typesetting Ltd
London SE1
Printed and bound in
Great Britain at
The Pitman Press, Bath
for the Publishers B. T. Batsford Ltd,
4 Fitzhardinge Street, London W1H 0AH

Contents

List of Illustrations

Acknowledgments

The Author and Publisher would like to thank the following for permission to use their photographs: French Government Tourist Office for Plates 1, 4, 5, 7, 8, 13-15, 17-21; Mrs I. M. Fresson for Plate 9; A. Moretti for Plates 2, 3, 10, 12; and J. Allan Cash Ltd for 6, 11, 16, 22-24.

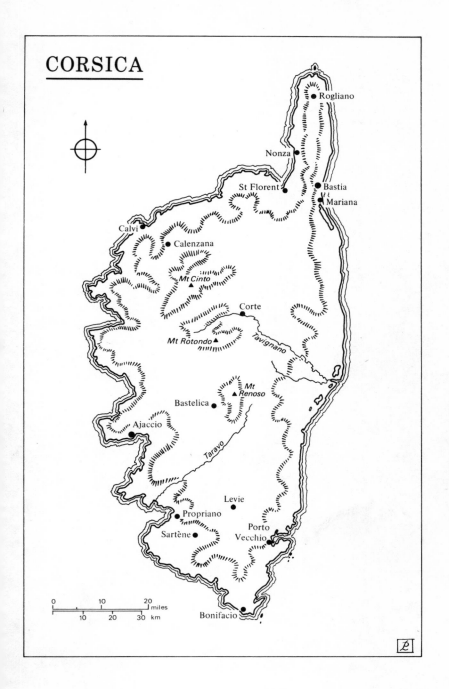

CORSICA

Rogliano

Nonza

St Florent • Bastia
Mariana

Calvi
Calenzana

Mt Cinto

Corte

Mt Rotondo

Tavignano

Mt Renoso

Bastelica

Ajaccio

Taravo

Levie

Propriano
Porto
Vecchio
Sartène

Bonifacio

0   10   20 miles
10   20   30 km

1 Genoa

Many centuries before the Christian era, a Ligurian peasant woman named Corsa saw one of her favourite heifers wander down to the sea shore, plunge into the rippling waves, and begin to swim towards the southern horizon. Without thinking, Corsa began to swim after her, and both must have been exceptionally strong swimmers as they did not stop till they reached the shores of an island, which the woman named Corsica.

There are, however, less fanciful accounts of how the island acquired its name. According to Louis Boell, it was originally named Cornea, and this would seem to be confirmed by an ancient study of Phonecian geography which states 'This island (Ichnusa) situated not far from Sardinia was first called Cornea, later Cyrnos, after the arrival of the Greeks'. Other Greek sources claim that after the fall of Troy, a Trojan noble called Corso sought refuge in Carthage. He then proceeded to show his gratitude by seducing Sica, one of the Queen's nieces. Obliged to fly from the kingdom, the couple reached an island which after their (eventual) marriage they named Corsica.

Whatever may be the true origin, it was the Greeks who first brought the island into the orbit of the civilized world. In *De Consolatione,* written during an eight-year exile in Corsica, Seneca wrote 'This country was inhabited in turn by different people leaving its beginning in the mists of antiquity. It is enough to say that the Greeks who are today established at

11

Massilia (Marseille) stopped here on their journey from their country.' He does not go on to explain why they did not remain, but it is likely that the commercially-minded Greeks did not consider that trade with the locals would be a worthwhile enterprise, and it was not till the sixth century BC, that the first Greek colony was founded at Alalia (564 BC), later Aleria, on the east coast near the mouth of the Tavignano river. They did not stay long to appreciate the pleasures of *L'Ile de Beauté*. A naval defeat made them change their minds about the island's salubrity. There was a general exodus, and it was not till 453 BC that they came back to re-found Alalia, and to introduce those two staple elements of Mediterranean life, the olive and the vine. They remained for over a century, but with only ninety miles separating the island from the mainland of the Italian peninsula, it was inevitable that they should eventually be drawn into the long struggle between Rome and Carthage.

In 280 BC, the Carthaginians stormed Alalia, wishing to use it as a naval base. Twenty years later, they were driven out by the Romans who demolished ancient Alalia to found their own city of Aleria, serving both as a base for their own navy and as a bridgehead to overrun the whole island. The local tribesmen were not prepared to accept foreign domination without a fight, and as the Romans were busy on other fronts it was not till 163 BC that the last centre of resistance was overcome by which time the Romans had gained a healthy respect for the islanders' fighting qualities and innate ferocity.

Following their struggle against the Romans who eventually subjected them, the Corsicans enjoyed a long period of peace in their troubled and bloody history. Aleria prospered for nearly 200 years, becoming the principal port of call for vessels plying between Marseille, Piraeus, Carthage and the Balearic islands, as well as a centre of commerce exporting oil, wine, wax, cork, timber, and copper from the Matra mines. Though the rise of Ostia deprived the city of much of its trade, this basic prosperity did not end till the Pax Romana was shattered by successive waves of Barbarian invasions, and the island was overrun first by the Vandals, then by the Ostragoths.

It was during the Roman period that Christianity was introduced, its earlier days now crystallized in the stories of Corsica's two native martyrs Saint Devote and Saint Julie. Devote, daughter of a well-to-do Alerian merchant family, was only a very young girl when in 202 the Roman Prefect Barbarus arrived on the island, charged by the Emperor Septimus Severus to put down this subversive faith which denied imperial divinity. Dragged before Barbarus, Devote refused to offer a sacrifice to the Roman Gods, and was condemned to be flogged to death. A true Corsican, she was no patient sufferer forgiving her tormentors. With her dying breath she cursed the Prefect, calling him 'the greatest scoundrel of all times and the worshipper of all the demons'.

The Vandals were responsible for Julie's violent death. Born in Carthage about the year 420, she was sold as a slave when the Vandals captured the city in 439. After some years in Syria, she was shipped west to Nonza on Cap Corse, still a slave, and there became a convert to Christianity. Ordered to renounce her faith, she refused. The Vandals were not prepared to waste time in arguments. He breasts were ripped off with red hot pincers, and thrown over the cliffs. At the very place where they fell, the legend says, twin fountains sprang from the bare rock face.

THE RIVAL REPUBLICS

The Corsicans were happy, at first, when the Ostragoths were driven out by the forces of Byzantium in 533, but disillusion soon followed. Most historians agree that the 200 years of Byzantine occupation were a long nightmare. By the time Byzantium's influence had faded in the western Mediterranean the island was caught up in the agonies of another long and deadly struggle: that between the Christian powers of the mainland, and the Moslem Saracens of North Africa. From 704 the Saracens subjected the island to a series of devasting invasions, reducing the population by almost ninety per cent, and it was the 300 years of Moslem terror that, in the view of Xavier Poli (1861-1923), author of *La Corse dans l'Antiquité et Haut Moyen Age,* forged the Corsican character. 'Driven from the coast and valleys' he says 'the Moslem killed the islanders' love of work by making work impossible . . . The individual could only count on himself, his own force, to fight the invader. From his eagle's nest in the mountains, he did not hesitate to swoop down to plunder. A whole mass of little independent clans were formed, often becoming bitter enemies. Deprived of a central direction, the individual became at the same time judge, executioner, and undisputed master of his entourage. He acquired thus an extraordinary gift of command and an unique spirit of intrigue . . .'

In 755 Pepin le Bref, son of Charles Martel, placed the island under Papal protection. This protection was purely nominal, and it was not till the Saracens suffered a series of crushing defeats both on land and at sea at the hands of the Republics of Pisa and Genoa, that the Moslem yoke was finally thrown off. Worn out not only by Saracen depredations, but also by periodical slaughter resulting from clan rivalry, the Corsicans turned to the Pope for a solution to their problems. In response to their appeal, Gregory VII decided to entrust the island to the care of Landolfo, Bishop of Pisa. To give added weight to his authority, the Pope made Landolfo an Archbishop, and increased the number of bishoprics in Corsica from four to six – Aleria, Ajaccio, Accia, Mariana, Nebbio and Sagona.

Pisa's tenure, however, was not to the liking of the rival Republic of Genoa. The Genoese Senate bombarded the Pope with complaints till, in 1193 Innocent II ceded them the bishoprics of Mariana, Nebbio and Accia, at the same time upgrading the Bishop of Genoa to Archbishop, thus putting the two republics on an equal ecclesiastic footing.

Far from being satisfied by this compromise, the Genoese looked upon this step as a beginning of the manoeuvre to oust their rival from the island altogether. They bided their time, and on the first Sunday of the new century, landed a powerful force at Bonifacio, on the island's southernmost tip facing

Sardinia, when most of the inhabitants were either inside or gathered round the principal church. Surprise was total. The town fell after offering only a token resistance. Masters in the art of fortification, it was not long before the Genoese had converted the town into a quasi-impregnable bastion and perfect shelter for the first Genoese colony, officially recognized in 1217 by the Pope Honorius II.

As was to be expected, Pisan reaction was violent. The Bonifacio incident started off a long war between the two republics, in which the native Corsicans joined to make the struggle tripartite. The early stages produced the first of Corsica's great leaders Sinucello della Rocca, a member of the most important of the Corsican 'great families', the Cinarchesi.

One cannot say that Sinucello showed great consistency of character or policy. Though siding first with the Genoese, as a true Corsican patriot, he could not tolerate their prolonged occupation of Bonifacio. Crossing to Italy, he offered his services to Pisa, and returning to the island with Pisan backing, raised a large force of Corsicans. At the head of his native army, he defeated the Genoese in a series of minor but hard-fought engagements. Nevertheless, convinced that the Genoese were the stronger of the two republics, he tried again to come to terms.

Despite their setbacks, the Genoese were by then firmly established not only in Bonifacio, but in Calvi and most of the north west of the island. Realising that their ambition was nothing short of total occupation, Sinucello broke off talks, and in 1264 set up a *Consulta* – an assembly of the heads of leading families – in which he proclaimed Corsica an independent state under Pisan protection, and proceeded to draw up a Constitution. As chief of this experimental state, Sinucello showed himself to be so gifted an administrator and legislator, that his name of Sinucello was replaced by *Giudice* (Judge).

One popular story tells that after a victory over the Genoese, he agreed to return all captured married men to their homes, provided the wives came in person to claim their husbands. This operation was left to the charge of one of his nephews who was so struck by the beauty of one of the wives that he made it a condition that she spend the night with him prior to liberating the prisoner. Giudice got to hear of the bargain. Despite the sacrosanct nature of family ties, the amorous nephew was arrested, summarily tried, and speedily executed. Giudice was not a man to be trifled with: he had the eyes of the dead Genoese torn out, salted, and sent in a pannier, to the Doge. On another occasion, furious that his amorous advances had been rejected by a pretty young widow, he had her seized and thrown into a cell to be kept for 'the pleasure of his soldiers and serfs'.

Clan – or family – rivalry was responsible for Giudice's downfall. The Giovanninellos, styling themselves as Barons, were deeply jealous of the della Roccas deserved popularity and position. More concerned with their own spite than their country's destiny, they staged a 'night of the long knives' in the course of which some seventy della Roccas and their friends were massacred, after which the Giovanninellos went over en bloc to the Genoese.

With Pisa's backing, however, Giudice was able to maintain his position, but in 1284 occurred a major disaster. The power of Pisa was smashed, never to recover, at the great naval battle of Meloria. The Pisans lost their entire fleet, some 5000 dead, and over 1000 were taken prisoner. 'If you want to see a Pisan these days' said one writer 'you have to make a tour of Genoa's prisons.' In the subsequent treaty, Pisa was obliged to renounce all her rights to Corsica and declare Giudice's rule illegal. Though a very old man, Giudice was able to beat off two Genoese offensives, but more and more Corsicans were being won over by the Giovanninellos including one of Giudice's illegitimate sons, Salnese who led his father into an ambush. Taken prisoner, Giudice was shipped over to Genoa and thrown into the Malapaga jail where, infirm and half blind, he died in 1312 at the age of ninety-eight.

With no inspired leader, Corsican resistance to the Genoese gradually evaporated. The Republic's domination was firmly established and was to last despite frequent bloody revolutions

1 AJACCIO; general view

interspersed with brief, intoxicating moments of independence till 1769.

These early days of Genoese rule witnessed two purely local revolutionary movements; the one aimed at the authority of the Church, the other at that of the Barons. In both these movements one finds what may be, in the words of contemporaries, history's first use of the term 'communist'.

The ecclesiastical revolt was embodied in a sect calling themselves the Giovannali (not to be confused with the Giovanninello family). Older writers mostly condemn them out of hand and shed no tears over their grisly fate but some of our contemporaries are inclined to view them with an almost sympathetic eye. The sect was supposedly formed by two illegitimate sons of a nobleman, Paola and Arrighi, and became dubbed 'communists' because members made a common pool of all their possessions, including wives and children. In the words of a scandalized chronicler – 'At night they would gather in their temple, and after a ceremony whose object was to "fortify" their stupid beliefs and ignoble doctrines, put out the lights and then and there, in the darkness, indulge in the most infamous orgies.'

Their suppression was ordered by the Pope, then at Avignon. A force described as 'an Army Corps' was despatched to the island, landed at Aleria and advancing inland surprised the Giovannali in their hide-out in the Alesani valley. The sectarians were exterminated but 'much to everyone's horror and surprise, amongst the corpses were found those of a number of noblemen'.

The protest against the grip of the feudal Barons was led by a man called Sambucuccio d'Alando. Raising an army mostly composed of villagers, he defeated the Barons and their retainers. Many look upon him as a traitor, because he came to an agreement with the Genoese, accepting their nominal rule provided they allowed local government to remain entirely in Corsican hands, but as Sambucuccio saw it, and with some justification, the remote control of Genoa was preferable, as far as the ordinary citizen was concerned, to the grinding oppression of the Barons and the bloody feuds their

2 Old street in AJACCIO.

constant quarrels – or vendettas – provoked.

Sambucuccio's fief covered only a portion of the island territory, that known as the *En-deça des Monts (Diqui dei Monti),* and this he welded into a single administrative unit to be known as *La Terra di Commune,* though the south remained firmly in the hands of the all-powerful Cinarchesi. The idea behind the Commune was to bring the villages of a region into contact with one another, since largely due to the terrain they had till then lived completely isolated existences. At Sambucuccio's instigation, villages were grouped into an 'ecclesiastical unit', known as a *Pieve.* Each *Pieve* being subdivided into *paesi* (villages) run by assemblies consisting of every adult inhabitant, including women, whose meeting place was the church. The assemblies, totally autonomous where local affairs were concerned, yearly elected a chief *Podesta* who, advised by a group of elders known as the *Padri del Commune,* had the responsibility of a final decision in any local problem or dispute. Controlling all the *Pieve,* where overall policy was concerned, was a 'Council of Twelve', *I Dodici.*

It is on this short-lived experiment that Corsicans claim that they were the first Europeans of modern times to devise a genuine democracy, which, but for outside intervention, might well have endured to the present day. Sambucuccio, however, seems to have neglected the vital aspect of defence. The Barons, fearing that the ideas of the Commune might prove contagious, attacked, overrunning the whole area, and forcing Sambucuccio to flee to Genoa to beg for help. He was never to return. In 1370, an outbreak of plague ravaged the Mediterranean lands, one of its victims being Sambucuccio. It is doubtful whether the Commune would have continued for long despite popular assertions as its principles did not suit the feudal mentality of the average villager.

The Genoese grip re-tightened, only to be loosened by another member of the della Rocca family, Arrigo, towards the end of the century. When Arrigo's father was killed in a clash with the Genoese, his family took refuge at the Court of the King of Aragon, to whom the Pope Boniface VII had ceded his rights to both Corsica and Sardinia, a cession which, however, the Genoese Senate refused to recognize. The Aragonese monarchs had shown no wish to become involved in a war with the powerful Republic over the question of the island, but in 1370 the King, Alfonso, gave his blessing and limited aid to Arrigo, when the latter proposed that he should land in Corsica and raise the standard of revolt.

Even Arrigo was surprised at the extent of his own success. Rival families rallied to his flag, and though ill-armed and untrained, the 'patriots' defeated the Genoese in battle after battle till the whole of the island, with the exception of fortress cities like Calvi and Bonifacio, were in their hands.

Proclaiming the island an independent state under Aragonese tutelage, he reigned for four years exercising absolute power, and with such severity that Barons and villagers alike began to ask themselves whether the foreign tyranny was not, of the two, the less oppressive. A revolt by the Counts of Cap Corse was easily and ruthlessly crushed, as was a second uprising supported by a Genoese contingent, but shortly afterwards Arrigo had to face an even larger Genoese expedition whose ranks were considerably swelled by local malcontents.

A series of bloody encounters went against him, forcing him to fly to Spain. Two months later, however, he was back on Corsican soil, turned the tables on the Genoese, captured the Genoese Governor and, greatest triumph of all, stormed the two reputedly impregnable fortresses of Calvi and Bonifacio. His successful career was cut short abruptly. In 1401 he was suddenly seized with violent stomach pains, dying in agony within twenty-four hours; the work, it is generally conceded, of a professional poisoner.

ARAGON AND THE BANK

When the Genoese felt that the Aragonese at last intended to assert their legal rights over Corsica, they offered their *de facto* authority to the French King, Charles VI. This offer was accepted by Charles who, nevertheless appointed a Genoese nobleman, by the name of Lomellino, to rule the island in his name, giving him the title of Count of Corsica, a move strongly resented by both Corsicans and Aragonese alike.

For the Aragonese, the rebuff was a serious insult, but the policy of not committing purely Spanish forces on a Corsican adventure still persisted. Thus they were all the more delighted to engage the services of another Corsican, Vincentello d'Istria, a direct descendant of Giudice della Rocca and nephew of the late Arrigo. Vincentello had exiled himself to Sardinia rather than submit to the dictates of Arrigo's illegitimate son Francesco, who claimed to be chief of the clan and demanded absolute obedience from every member of both the Cinarca and Istria families. In Sardinia, Vincentello equipped a small but fast vessel and with a few companions soon became the terror of the Genoese in the neighbourhood of Bonifacio. Invited as a result of these exploits to the Aragonese Court, he made a deep impression on the King who offered full backing for a major expedition against Genoese-held Corsica.

Reading that the King was won over by the Corsican's charm, one is forced to the conclusion that he must have been possessed of a remarkable personality, for there is nothing charming about the physical description left by the historian Giovanni della Grossa who knew him well. 'He was very tall' says della Grossa 'but his arms were small and so curved that he could not stretch them out to their full length. His fingers were short, thick, spatulate. His face was as lined as that of an old woman, but lit up by magnificent black eyes. An enormous wart, near his nose and under his right eyelid, gave the impression that his eye had fallen from its socket and was hanging down. He had thick legs and a powerful chest, taken all round, his person did not lack charm.' He was also very much a 'ladies man' with as many victories to his credit 'in the courts of Venus as on the field of Mars'.

Landing in Corsica with a small force of Spanish troops, Vincentello was able to rally the overwhelming majority of his fellow countrymen, and to the battle cry of *'Cinarchesi ed Aragona'*, drove the Genoese and their ally, the angry Francesco della Rocca, back to their fortresses. In June 1407, a Consulta proclaimed him as 'the true Count of Corsica,' and in February 1408, with the fall of Bastia, the island was declared to be an apanage of the King of Aragon with Vincentello as his representative. In the late autumn, however, Francesco and the reinforced Genoese returned to the attack. Vincentello was wounded, his army scattered, and he himself forced to take refuge in Sicily.

A year later he was back again, landing this time near Ajaccio, and receiving the same enthusiastic welcome from the local population. In a major battle near Biguglia, he was not only victorious, but in the melée he sought out and killed his cousin Francesco, thus ridding himself of his bitterest enemy. War against the Genoese continued on a minor scale for the next six years, but as no Aragonese reinforcements were forthcoming, the territory held by the loyal Corsicans was gradually compressed into an ever diminishing perimeter.

In 1416, however, the ambitious and talented Alfonso V, succeeded to the throne on the death of the rather apathetic Ferdinand. One of his first acts was to invite Vincentello to Saragossa and bestow on him the title of Viceroy of Corsica, assuring him that massive reinforcements would be despatched in the near future to wipe out the last Genoese centres of resistance. Full of confidence Vincentello returned to the island to speed up operations. In the campaign that followed he showed himself to be a worthy precursor of Napoleon. After a series of lightning moves, surprise raids, and well-laid ambushes, he routed and destroyed the combined Genoese and pro-Genoese Corsican forces in the neighbourhood of Biguglia. Resistance collapsed, the whole island with the sole exceptions of Calvi and Bonifacio falling into his hands. (In 1418, Vincentello gave orders for the building of Corte citadel, as a rival, purely Corsican stronghold.)

The victory delighted Alfonso encouraging him to break a long established tradition. No King of Aragon had ever set foot on Corsican soil, so that Vincentello was surprised to learn that Alfonso would be coming in person to supervise the attack on Calvi and Bonifacio.

He arrived in September 1420 with a veritable armada;

thirteen galleons, twenty-three triremes, and a swarm of troop transports. The sight of such a display of might so awed the Calvi garrison that the city was surrendered without a shot being fired. The defenders of Bonifacio, however, were made of considerably sterner stuff. Though attacked both by the Spanish fleet from the sea and by Vincentello's triumphant army from the land, they were determined to hold out to the last man, a determination equally shared by the civilian population. Their courage was phenomenal. Food soon ran short; there were incidents of plague; bombardments and attacks were furious and insistent, but there was no thought of surrender. Priests, women, even children, took their places on the ramparts shoulder to shoulder with the troops.

Fortunately for the defenders, by the New Year, Alfonso was getting tired of so static a situation, furthermore, his thoughts were turning from Corsica to Naples where the Queen, Jeanne II, attacked by the Franco-Genoese, had offered him the throne in return for armed help. For him Naples was a far more glittering prize than an island of notoriously rebellious inhabitants. To Vincentello's despair, the Spaniards sailed south, leaving him with no choice other than to raise the siege.

Nevertheless, he was still Viceroy and master of the whole of Corsica with the exception of the one citadel. And such was the power of his name that he was able to maintain his position, after making a 'political' marriage with the daughter of the Marquis Gentile of Nonza, thus assuring himself of the allegiance of most of the independent-minded Cap Corse noble families, for the next fourteen years.

It might have been for longer, had he not committed an incredible act of folly which would have damned him in most countries, but which in Corsica was the equivalent of suicide. 'Vincentello' says Giovanni della Grossa 'seized by force a young girl belonging to one of the principal families of the land and forced her openly to share his bed; a deed truly unworthy of so great a man, unworthy of his past glory and his power; because he who cannot vanquish his passions, cannot in all truth call himself victorious'. To make matters worse, the kidnapped girl was already engaged. Popular fury, we are told, reached an unparalleled height, and was hardly appeased when Vincentello suddenly decided to double taxation. Corsicans from every level of society rose up against 'the tyrant'.

Realising too late his mistakes, Vincentello hired a small boat and tried to reach Sardinia. A violent storm blew his vessel northwards towards the Provençal coast, and then, the wind changing freakishly, back towards the western shores of Corsica, where it was intercepted and captured by Vincentello's brother, Giovanni, with whom he had quarrelled violently some months previously. Giovanni offered to help his brother's escape, but shortly afterwards, the two small Corsican vessels were engaged by a powerful Genoese galley. Giovanni got away – some suspect that he had deliberately led his brother into an ambush – but Vincentello's craft was boarded, and Vincentello taken in chains to Genoa.

The Genoese lost no time in ridding themselves of one of their most dangerous opponents. Tried by the Grand Council of the Republic, Vincentello was condemned to death and beheaded on the steps of the Doge's palace by the *Mannaja*, a forerunner of the guillotine.

For the next few years, the Genoese, reinstated in all the main towns, firmly holding the coast, were content to sit back and watch the great families draining Corsican blood in senseless vendettas, but as the struggle with both Venice and the Turks grew more acute, they appointed the Bank (or Office) of Saint George – a privately owned Genoese Bank – to rule the island under their nominal protection. The Bank was an extraordinary institution: almost a state within the state, often referred to as a 'Financial Republic', maintaining its own Senate and its own armed forces.

Its temporary domination of the island was even more oppressive than that of Genoa proper. Anxious to make the venture pay vast profits, the Bank was extortionate in the extreme in its attempt to raise and enforce payment of taxes. Within a year of their taking over, the Bank's officials had to face a revolt led by Raffé de Leca, soon to be notorious for the atrocities carried out on his orders. The Bank's general,

Antonio Calvo, riposted with equal brutality, and when in
1456 de Leca was captured, he was first hideously tortured
before being hanged in the company of his twenty-two
brothers. As a final horror, the Bank announced a general
amnesty (1458) for its principal opponents, the Cinarca
family, inviting them to a banquet to celebrate the 'coming of
peace'. After having wined and dined exceedingly well, they
were seized by a group of armed men suddenly bursting in,
and beheaded on the spot. One wonders whether it was this
story which inspired one of Al Capone's better-known
Chicago massacres.

The Bank's rule ended in 1463 when the Duke of Milan,
having become master of Genoa, forced it to cede its rights,
but thirteen years later after throwing off Milan's yoke, the
Genoese reassumed control.

THE AGE OF THE HEROES

As the century drew to its close, the struggle between Corsican
patriots and Genoese would-be colonizers, entered an even
more bitter stage, the Genoese being led by the first of the
famous Doria family, Andrea, the Corsicans by Giampolo
(Gian' Paolo) de Leca, and yet another della Rocca, Rinuccio.
It is a sad thought that had these two brave men combined
their efforts from the beginning, the Genoese might well have
been driven out, but when Giampolo issued his first call to
arms, jealousy led Rinuccio to offer his services to the enemy,
and it was not till the patriots had been defeated at Foce al
Sorbo, Giampolo being forced to flee leaving his son, Orlando,
in Genoese hands, that Rinuccio had a Saint Paul-like
revelation, from then on devoting his whole life to the cause of
Corsican independence.

His first campaign was as ill-fated as that of Giampolo. His
patriot army was heavily defeated by the brilliant Andrea
Doria, as capable a general as he was admiral. In 1504, he and
all his family were captured, deported, and interned in Genoa
itself. Rinuccio soon managed to escape, leaving his family to
the ruthless Genoese, and eventually reaching Sardinia where
Giampolo was living in exile. One does not know whether

Giampolo was discouraged by his earlier failure, whether he was unable to trust a man who had once borne arms against him, or whether he felt that the struggle against Genoa was hopeless and could only add to the people's already great suffering, but whatever the reason, he refused to contemplate further adventures.

In spite of this setback, however, and determining to go it alone, Rinuccio landed in Corsica with only eighteen followers, unmoved, apparently by the news that his wife and children had been thrown into a dungeon.

The Genoese had no difficulty in routing Rinuccio's peasant rabble, and to show that he meant to stamp out any form of rebellion pitilessly, Andrea Doria sent orders to Genoa for Rinuccio's eldest son to be beheaded. Flight to Sardinia, thence to Spain, was followed by a second, equally abortive landing. Again a prisoner, Rinuccio once more found himself in a Genoese cell lucky to retain his head. Yet three years later he contrived a daring escape and again appeared on Corsican soil with a handful of adventurers.

Doria's policy of retaliation and scorched earth had, however, borne fruit. To the islanders Rinuccio had become a symbol of misfortune. They were not prepared to betray him, but equally only a negligible few were prepared to march with him. In a blundering attempt to regain prestige, Rinuccio and his band ambushed and massacred a small Genoese detachment, then fled to the mountains. A massive manhunt was promptly organized, lasting several weeks till, on 11 May 1511, Rinuccio himself was cornered and killed after a short but fierce resistance.

Though one of the island's legendary 'heroes', Rinuccio had in fact done nothing to aid Corsican independence. On the contrary, his ill-organized sedition had brought unprecedented misery in its wake. Andrea Doria was merciless. Apart from the usual horrors of conflict in those days – arson, massacre of non-combatants, pillage, deliberate destruction of crops, epidemics, starvation – even those in remoter areas not actually involved in the fighting faced disaster because of the total collapse of the island's economy.

The result was massive emigration to the mainland, or 'continent' as the Corsicans called it – and still do. Those who emigrated had no skills to offer other than an inborn proficiency in the handling of arms combined with a remarkable moral and physical toughness. It was natural, therefore, that they should seek recruitment in the service of whoever was prepared to pay the highest wage, and it is from this time that Corsicans began to figure so prominently as mercenaries in 'continental' armies.

2 Sampiero Corso

One of the young men who had left home to serve on the continent was a certain Sampiero, native of the village of Bastelica, in the mountains to the north east of Ajaccio. Although one of Corsica's greatest 'heroes', there is no definite record of his family name. All that is known for certain is that he was a shepherd's son. Employed in the service of Prince Giovanni di Medici, it was not long before he enjoyed the Prince's confidence as an outstandingly brave and skilful soldier. In 1522, now one of the Prince's most trusted commanders, he took part in the campaigns of the famous French king, François I, distinguishing himself particularly in the battles of Romagnano and Pavia.

In November 1526, near Mantua, Giovanni de Medici was badly wounded and died a few days later.

Sampiero continued to serve the French king, until in 1545, after so many years of distinguished service with a foreign power, his thoughts began to turn to his native island. He was forty-seven years old, unmarried with no heir to carry on his name which was now a byword in military circles. Granted leave, he returned to Corsica for the sole purpose of finding a wife. Eventually his choice fell on the only daughter of one of the great families who had been so hard hit by the recent wars: Vannina (Giovannina) d'Ornano, only just fifteen years old. Her father, Francesco was happy to forget his future son-in-law's humble origin and the fact that he was more than thirty years older than his prospective bride, seeing in this already legendary warrior the one man capable of leading a campaign to throw the Genoese into the sea.

Shortly after the wedding, Sampiero paid a visit to Bastia. The Genoese Governor, thinking along the same lines as Francesco d'Ornano, trumped up an excuse to arrest him and throw him into the local jail. Francesco, however, could count on influential friends on the mainland, and was able to obtain the personal intervention of the French King Henri II to secure his son-in-law's release.

The Governor's stupid action was to cost Genoa dear. Outraged at such treatment, Sampiero vowed that he would never rest till the last Genoese had been driven from, or buried in, Corsican soil.

The fulfilment of this new-found ambition was greatly aided by the European political situation, dominated as it was by the rivalry existing between Henri II of France, and the Emperor Charles V. For both these monarchs, Corsica had become an important pawn in the power game.

Allied with the Turks, Henri II, considered the island would provide excellent harbour facilities for the combined Turco-French fleet, and at the same time since Andrea Doria, now Doge of Venice, had broken with France to embrace the cause of the Emperor, its loss would strike a severe blow to enemy prestige as well as depriving them of a naval base from which to harass the French coast. At a conference held at Castiglione, under the aegis of the French commander, the Maréchal de Thermes, Sampiero assured those present that the moment the first French troops landed, the islanders, as one man, would flock to their standards to join in the fight against the detested Genoese.

An expedition was mounted in 1553, Sampiero being joined by an eager crowd of Corsican exiles, the majority mercenaries. As promised, his appearance alone inspired the citizens of Bastia to open the gates to the invaders. Leaving behind a small occupying force, the Maréchal then split his army into four columns, that led by Sampiero being given the citadel of Corte as its objective. Thanks to its natural position and well-planned defences, Corte should have been able to hold out indefinitely, but, like Bastia, surrendered without firing a shot. Its fall was soon followed by that of Ajaccio.

Within a few days, the whole of the island with the exception of Calvi and Bonifacio, was in French hands, their lightning victory due almost entirely to Sampiero and his Corsicans.

Bonifacio fell to a ruse, but Calvi resisted every assault, thus giving the Genoese time to assemble a relief force of over 12,000 men, which landed in the region of Saint Florent, at the western foot of Cap Corse. By this time the Maréchal and Sampiero were on strained terms. Never a dynamic personality, the French leader refused to try to regain the initiative, even when Andrea Doria, commanding the invading force, had made a triumphal re-entry into Bastia. Exasperated, Sampiero decided to ignore his superior's orders to remain on the defensive, and gathering together a scratch force of Corsicans, attacked the Genoese at Vescovato. The battle was bloody but indecisive, Sampiero himself receiving a severe wound in the leg. Though in great pain, he refused to leave the field and shortly afterwards again encountered the Genoese in the region of the Col de Tenda, inflicting on them one of the most decisive defeats in the long history of the island's wars with the Republic.

Instead of congratulating him, the Maréchal de Thermes accused Sampiero of insubordination, had him put under arrest, and returned to France where he had a short spell in prison before being released on the personal order of Catherine de Medici. Returning as quickly as possible to Corsica, he found that de Thermes himself had been dismissed, and on popular demand, the island placed under the protection of the King of France. 'In order to remove all doubt from your minds, and all hope from the Genoese' ran the proclamation 'the King has incorporated this island in the French Crown, something which he has never done for any other of his provinces. This incorporation binds you irrevocably to the French kingdom, and the King will not abandon you any more than he would abandon his own crown.'

Yet only two years later, in 1559, to the utter dismay of every Corsican, news was received that the two super powers, France and Spain, had decided to make peace, and that one of

the clauses of the treaty of Cateau Cambrésis which brought
hostilities to an end, stated that Henri of France agreed to
hand back Corsica to Genoa.

According to the German historian, Doctor F. Gregorovius
'So cruel a blow wrung an immense cry of despair from the
Corsican nation's heart, to which all its valiant children were
to respond with their usual unquenchable ardour.'

Foremost of those to 'respond' was Sampiero, of whom a
contemporary has left a striking picture as he was then, in late
middle age. 'Tall, his features clear cut, his general
demeanour proud and haughty. His beard was darkish
brown, his hair black and wavy, his look bright and
penetrating, his speech brief, concise, yet impassioned;
though only a rugged son of nature without any basic
education, he was possessed of a high degree of intelligence
and a remarkable power of judgment . . . he lived modestly
and soberly after the manner of the mountain shepherds, clad
in the roughest cloth worn by those accustomed to sleep in the
open air. Though he had sojourned in the world's most
sumptuous courts, Florence and Paris, he had absorbed
nothing either of their physical decadence or their corrupt
morals '

Though profoundly disillusioned by France's betrayal, he
determined to try to plead his long and distinguished service
to the crown to persuade the monarch not to wash his hands
completely of the land he had promised to protect. A quick
journey to Paris only resulted in further, more bitter,
deception. Though welcomed at the Court, he was unable to
obtain even a vague promise of help. Perceiving that if ever
Corsica were to rid herself of the Genoese, another powerful
ally must be found to replace defaulting France, he left the
French capital to begin a long, heartbreaking odyssey which
took him to every petty Italian state, across the Mediterranean
to Algiers, and eventually to Constantinople, to the Court of
the Sultan Suliman II.

Wherever he went, it was the same discouraging,
despairing, story. He was received with great courtesy,
listened to with equally great sympathy, but quite unable to

interest any of the rulers, great or small, in coming to the aid of his beloved homeland. No one was prepared to risk open conflict with Genoa who could count on the support of one, possibly of both, the super powers. Oppressed Corsica had nothing material to offer as the price of friendship.

THE CORSICAN OTHELLO

Meanwhile, the Genoese who were as versed in the art of intrigue as they were in the purely martial skills, were constantly on the look-out for some way to destroy their principal enemy, who seemed to enjoy a charmed life on the battlefield.

During Sampiero's prolonged absence, Genoese attentions turned to his wife Vannina, temporarily settled in Marseille with her younger son Francesco, while the elder, Alfonso, was serving in the French *Garde Royale*. It was then that some anonymous master of psychology, resisting suggestions that wife and younger son might be conveniently liquidated, pointed out that their violent death would only serve to inspire Sampiero to greater prodigies of valour whereas if it could be made to appear that his wife had betrayed him, outraged sense of honour might well come near to depriving him of his reason.

After much deliberation and careful planning the plotters enlisted the aid of two men, implicitly trusted alike by Sampiero and Vannina. These were Agosto Bazzicalupa and a priest, Michelangelo Ombrone, agreed to approach Vannina with the suggestion that she and Francesco proceed to Genoa, to discuss with representatives of the Republic possible terms for a durable peace.

The two men did their work so well, that when Vannina, persuaded that the destiny of Corsica was in her hands, embarked for Genoa, she turned to the friends who had come to wave her farewell, saying 'Ah dear God! Now we will be able to live in peace, all be happy, and it will be thanks to me.'

Sampiero was actually in Algiers when the Genoese managed to pass on the information that his wife and younger son were on the point of embarking of their own free will, for

Genoa. As the conspirators expected, he immediately leaped to the conclusion that he had been betrayed. His first impulse was to abandon everything and set sail for Marseille, but perversely his exaggerated sense of honour and duty, held him back. He had sworn to complete this ally-searching tour of the Mediterranean, and nothing, therefore, must stand in the way of its accomplishment. Broken heartedly – we are told – he sent in his place one of his closest friends, Antonio de San Fiorenza, to plead with Vannina to resist 'temptation', while he himself set sail for Constantinople.

Antonio departed immediately. The winds were favourable and he made the voyage in record time but, to his horror, he found on arrival at Marseille that Vannina had sailed a bare twenty-four hours earlier in the company of Bazzicalupa and Ombone. Losing no time, he chartered a boat and set off in pursuit. Luck was with him. On approaching Antibes, he overtook a small vessel flying the Genoese flag which he guessed was probably sheltering the amateur ambassador, and which he ordered to 'heave to' in 'the name of Sampiero and the King of France'.

Recognising Antonio, Vannina demanded to be transferred to his boat. Having no wish to be involved in an argument with a French crew in French waters, the Genoese obeyed, glad to be rid of so potentially dangerous a passenger.

Within minutes, Antonio saw plainly that Vannina had been tricked by the two men she felt were most to be trusted in her husband's absence, but at the same time he knew his master only too well. Age had not made Sampiero more approachable, more mentally supple, or understanding. For some time he had been voicing his fears that the difference in their ages might be causing his wife to dream of a younger man's embraces. Above all he was not a man even to listen where he felt 'honour' was involved.

Convinced that Vannina's life was in danger, San Fiorenza suggested she place herself under the protection of the Bishop of Aix. The Bishop, however, unwilling to interfere in so delicate a matter, suggested referring the matter to the Aix parliament. At this point Vannina came to a decision which

was to prove fatal. She was well aware she had been the dupe of the Genoese, she told Antonio, but having acted in all good faith, her conscience was clear. This being the case, she was more than willing to accept the consequences. She would go to Aix, but as a private individual, refusing any form of official protection. 'I am' she said 'the wife of Sampiero, and whatever he wills of me I bow to his will'. Nothing could make her change her mind, and it was in a chateau near the city, that the strained little party awaited the frustrated hero's return.

Soured by the failure of his mission, tortured by the self-conjured picture of his wife's 'betrayal', the Corsican leader was in the blackest of moods when at last he disembarked at Marseille. Arriving at the chateau he could not bring himself to confront his wife, and spent the whole night pacing up and down the grounds refusing food and drink, not allowing Antonio to utter a single word.

As day broke his mind appeared made up. With Antonio always at his heels he strode up the steps and into the hall where Vannina was already waiting to greet him. After a brief silence as the two faced each other, Sampiero announced that they would be returning to Marseille immediately. Not a word was spoken on the way. No one, not even Antonio, dared approach Sampiero as he rode well ahead of the rest of the party. Later Antonio recorded that he hoped his master's fury 'would at least drop below boiling point to allow me a moment to reveal the truth'.

He was never given the opportunity.

As they entered the deserted Marseille house, the little control Sampiero had exercised, snapped. Still terrifyingly silent, he turned on Vannina forcing her to kneel at his feet, then murmuring something about 'forgiving her for her sins', strangled her.

There is no doubt that till the day of his death, Sampiero was satisfied that he had acted in the only possible way compatible with his honour. Whether anyone ever tried to point out to him that he had cruelly misjudged his wife is not recorded, but never, at any time, did he ever show, or hint at, the slightest feelings of remorse for a brutal, senseless crime. It

5 *PIANA church*
6 les Calanches, *or Red Rocks*

was typical of him that after having staged an elaborate funeral for the wretched Vannina, he was off to Paris to plead once more for French aid in the 'liberation' of Corsica.

In Paris, his reception was frigid. News of the murder had preceded him. In the eyes of the Court he was nothing but a crude, savage, bandit; a common assassin. Pressure was put on the Monarch to have him arrested and executed. Neither the King, nor the Queen, however, could forget that he had in the past served France so well. Receiving him in private audience, they made it clear that, though they still wished him success, there could be no question of material aid in any form.

On the long ride south, in a sombre mood, Sampiero nevertheless came to an irrevocable decision. Though he had now given up all hope of an alliance, he would not give up his crusade. He would carry on alone; till death.

On 12 June 1564, accompanied by a tiny force of twenty Corsicans and twenty-five Frenchmen, he landed on Corsican soil after repeating the Roman gesture of burning the vessels which had carried them. With his handful of followers, he stormed the fortress of Istria, then, his ranks swelled to 200, marched against the Genoese army in the region of Corte. Such was the spell of his name that the city surrendered, his entry into the citadel being the signal for a mass uprising of the mountain villages. Two battles of exceptional ferocity were then fought with the Genoese army. In the second, near Ponte Nuovo, the Genoese were routed; 300, including their able general Nicolo Negri, were killed, over 2000 taken prisoner.

Corsicans who had been sitting on the fence now flocked to Sampiero's banner. By 25 July most of the island was his, and at a Consulta held at Levie, the heads of the great families acknowledged his leadership and swore an oath of allegiance. His triumph seemed complete, but, as so often in the past, Genoa stubbornly refused to admit défeat. A price of 4000 *écus* was put on Sampiero's head, while an expeditionary force of mixed German and Italian troops was rushed to the island under the command of another of the Dorias, Stefano. A typical Doria, Stefano combined high military talent with cold brutality.

The Corsicans were left in no doubt that his aim was nothing less than the extermination of the Corsican people. This he made clear in a manifesto:

> When the Athenians captured the town of Milo after a seven months' siege, every inhabitant over the age of fourteen was put to the sword, and to reinforce their conquest, they sent settlers to repopulate it. Why not follow their example? . . I may be accused of violating the laws of humanity and civilization; it does not worry me. All I wish is that the very mention of my name spreads terror. We must not hesitate to ravage the countryside, burn and raze to the ground the villages and any habitation guilty of sheltering the rebels.

Typical of Stefano's methods was the capture and torturing of the mother of one of Sampiero's ablest generals, Achille Campocasso. Campocasso managed to rescue her, but Stefano's cold-blooded action had the desired effect. To protect his mother from a similar ordeal in the future, Campocasso let it be known that he would take no further part in operations.

The ensuing campaigns were the most bloody to date in the island's history. Vast areas were laid waste, crops burned, entire flocks of sheep and herds of cattle had their throats cut, no less than 123 villages were razed to the ground. Sampiero's men responded in kind: 'Both sides carried out the most abominable atrocities, prisoners were mutilated, blinded, burnt alive, thrown to the dogs, etc.'

Finally Stefano Doria was decisively beaten in the Luminanda Gorges, a defeat which so shattered his morale that he asked to be relieved of his command, and was replaced by a man who was no commander, but a master of intrigue, named Fornari. It was he who persuaded the authorities of the Republic that rather than drain Genoese manpower in continuous and costly operations against the seemingly invincible Sampiero, it would be better to entail his destruction by more subtle means. *Morto Sampiero, tutti se chieteranno* (Sampiero dead, everybody will calm down) was his favourite saying.

The three d'Ornano brothers, Francesco, Antonio, and Michelangelo, were waiting for the first opportunity to avenge their sister's death. Fornari was soon in touch with them. Lavishly supplied with Genoese gold, the brothers managed to secure the co-operation of a monk from Bastelica (Sampiero's birthplace), Ambrosio, and of Sampiero's trusted groom, Vittolo, the plot being directed by a Genoese, colonel Rafaelle Giustiniani, who had set up a temporary headquarters in Ajaccio.

Finally after details had been worked out, the monk Ambrosio went to Sampiero with forged letters to the effect that heavy fighting had broken out in the neighbourhood of Roca where his presence was urgently needed. Sampiero saw no reason to doubt the message's authenticity, and though sixty-nine years old had lost none of his furious energy. Calling on Vittolo to saddle the horses, he announced that he would be heading for Roca by the shortest route, that which lay through the narrow Cavro valley. This information was immediately passed back to Ajaccio, so that by the time Sampiero and his small group which included his elder son, Alfonso, reached the head of the valley, Giustiniani, the d'Ornanos, and a strong mixed force of cavalry and infantry were already in position.

As soon as firing broke out, Sampiero realised that he had ridden into a trap. His first reaction was to order Alfonso to make good his escape so as to be able to carry on the fight. Unwilling to abandon his father, but too well disciplined to dispute orders, Alfonso was fortunate to be able to battle his way to safety, unscathed.

Slowly the ring closed, as one by one Sampiero's companions were struck down, leaving him alone in a circle of dead and dying, and the three brothers, who had insisted that he die by their hands, moved in for the kill. Antonio collapsed, hit in the head by a pistol shot. A second would certainly have killed him, but Vittolo had managed to extract the bullet. Throwing away the useless pistol, Sampiero turned to face

Francesco and Michelangelo, sword in hand. As their blades crossed, Vittolo crept up from behind and stabbed him in the back. Mortally wounded, Sampiero's body had barely touched the ground before Francesco had severed his head from his shoulders. One source claims that 'the corpse was carved up, and to avenge their comrades burnt alive on Sampiero's orders, the German mercenaries ate his entrails'.

This grisly detail may be an exaggeration, but in any case the brothers rode off with their bloody trophy as a present for the delighted Governor, Fornari. 'Thank God' wrote the latter to the Doge 'this morning I put the head of the rebel Sampiero on a stake at the entrance to Ajaccio, and one leg on the bastion . . .. '

Fornari, however, was disillusioned by the aftermath of the plot. Instead of collapsing automatically, as he had hoped, Corsican resistance was reinforced round the figure of their hero's son. Though only seventeen, Alfonso soon showed that he had inherited much of his father's bravura. For two years the war continued mercilessly, with varying fortune, till by 1569 both sides were exhausted.

It was this year that the scheming Fornari was replaced by Giorgio Doria, the only member of the family whose name does not awake bitter memories in Corsican hearts.

Giorgio's first act was to proclaim a general amnesty, and encouraged by the response to this gesture, as well as by Alfonso's agreement to an armistice, he then made genuine efforts to help the war-torn island's economy. For his part Alfonso, open-minded enough to realise that a period of peace was vital were Corsica to survive, persuaded 300 of the most ardent patriots to join him in voluntary exile, thus avoiding the temptation of breaking the much-needed truce.

Most of the 300 took up the traditional trade of mercenary soldier. Alfonso himself went to Paris, where the King gave him command of the Corsican Royal Guards; within a few years he had risen to the dignity of Marshal of France. One of his closest friends, Savelli, was made a Grandee of Spain, another, Vareli, became Governor of the Spanish Indies, while in Venice, a Pozzo di Borgo was the first of this family, later to be known as the Bonapartes, most implacable enemy, to carve for himself a name on the international screen.

3 The Long Night

It was unfortunate that Giorgio Doria's enlightened administration lasted so short a time, and that succeeding governors were imbued with the idea that the 'colony' should be milked dry for the benefit of the mother city. Mercilessly taxed, the people were kept in a state of semi-slavery The German, Gregorovius, also produces the alarming statistic that, in a period of just under thirty years, some 28,000 murders were recorded. Fratricidal violence suited the Genoese book. It killed off potential rebels, and provided a source of income, for the Genoese judges were always prepared to accept a cash payment to write off a murder as self-defence, and permission to own a lethal weapon, and the fine for failing to obtain such a permission was a constant boost for the Governor's treasury.

Hatred of the Genoese was fomented when, towards the end of the seventeenth century, a band of territory on the western side of the island was allotted to a group of Maniot Greeks fleeing from the Turks, with the promise of the Republic's protection against the depredations of the 'natives', and freedom of worship according to the Orthodox rites. But despite this further blow to national pride, the Corsicans were so weakened by eternal strife that the Greeks were able to settle in the face of negligible opposition, and it was not till 1727 that the population again resorted to arms, reviving memories of the heroic days of the Cinarchesi and Sampiero.

The actual rising was sparked off by an unusual combination of events. A Corsican conscript with the Genoese army on the mainland had, for a minor offence, been seated astride a wooden horse on the piazza, and exposed to the jeers and insults of the locals. This was more than a group of fellow Corsican conscripts could stand. They attacked the crowd. In the ensuing fracas a number of locals and conscripts were killed or seriously injured. The Genoese promptly disarmed and arrested every Corsican in the unit, whether or not he had been involved in the riot. Hauled up before a judge, every man was found guilty of attempted mutiny and executed.

News of this cold-blooded massacre reached Corsica the very day a new tax, known as the *Due Seini* came into force. In the area of Bozio, the tax collector, discovered that an elderly villager, named Cardone was half a *sou* short of the sum due and ordered him to pay up not later than the following morning, or else face a long term of imprisonment.

Cardone left for his home loudly bewailing his fate to everyone in sight, his distress finally changing to anger, and exhortations to all and sundry to rid themselves of the accursed foreign oppressor. His plight still further exacerbated feelings already running high at the thought of the executions. Suddenly there were cries of *Evviva la Liberta! Evviva il Populo!* As if by magic church bells began to ring, while messengers ran from village to village with the call to arms.

It was the beginning of a war that was to last forty years. As one man, the Corsicans refused to pay not only the *Due Seini*, but any Genoese imposed tax. Led by a villager named Pompiliani, the patriots forced a small Genoese column to fall back on Bastia, then, though still armed mostly with scythes and pitchforks, stormed Aleria, capturing vast stores of arms and ammunition. Marching on Bastia, Pompiliani was, perhaps, foolish to agree to a truce to discuss terms, a truce which gave the Genoese time to send over reinforcements. When the talks proved abortive, Pompiliani, certain that he would be able to take the city by storm, launched his first attack against the fort of Monserrato, commanding the southern approach. On 20 December Monserrato fell, leaving 400 prisoners and considerable material in Corsican hands.

At this point a certain mystery surrounds the person of

Pompiliani himself. Some claim that for some inexplicable reason he was relieved of his command, others that he was taken prisoner during the course of the battle, others that he was killed, but whichever of these solutions may be correct, the fact remains that from the moment of the capture of the fortress, his name disappears from the pages of history.

Two days later, however, a Consulta was held at San Pancrazio de Biguglia, at which having declared that life under Genoese tyranny could no longer be tolerated, every Corsican of an age to bear arms was called upon to swear never to rest till the 'foreign yoke had been finally and for ever shaken off', and three leaders elected and styled 'Generals of the Nation' – Luigi Giafferi, Filiberto Ciattoni, and Andrea Colonna Ceccaldi.

These three, unlike the rugged Sampiero, were highly educated men. Giafferi and Ciattoni had served as officers with the Corsican regiment of the Neapolitan army, while Ceccaldi, a doctor, had for a time been one of the *Dodici,* the nominally still existent Council of Twelve. Like Sampiero, however, they realised that outside help was vital, a realisation now shared by the Genoese.

In this search the Genoese were better placed than the islanders. Their ambassadors were on the spot, and most important of all, they had the money available to pay for foreign aid. In the end they were able to come to an agreement with the Emperor of Austria to hire 6000 infantrymen and a force of 2000 cavalry for a monthly payment of 30,000 florins, and a down payment of 100 florins for every man killed or seriously wounded. Dismay was tempered by a grim amusement when the Corsicans heard of this last, somewhat bizarre, clause. In future engagements, the patriots used to shout *Genova! Cento florini!* every time one of the Austrian contingent was seen to fall.

As soon as news of the outbreak of this new war for Corsican independence reached the mainland, the majority of the Corsican mercenaries hurried back to join in the fight. Their presence was invaluable. It was largely due to them, a solid cadre of trained and experienced fighting men, that the

Corsican 'generals' were able to hold up the combined Austro-Genoese forces under General Baron von Wachtendonck and Camillo Doria.

Operations had reached a near stalemate when, towards the end of 1731, Wachtendonck launched an offensive into the mountains of the Balanga region. It was a rash move, playing right into the Corsican's hands. In a terrain totally unsuited to cavalry or the manoeuvring of his infantry in parade ground formations, Wachtendonck soon found himself surrounded, and threatened with total annihilation, after suffering heavy casualties.

Though the Austrians were at his mercy, the Corsican commander, Luigi Giafferi, had the good sense to hold his men back from indulging in a wholesale slaughter of the demoralized Austrians. Instead he offered to parley, and in the course of his talks with Wachtendonck, offered the Baron his life, and that of his soldiers, if he would promise to agree to a two months' armistice, and to return immediately to Vienna to put Corsica's case before the Emperor.

Von Wachtendonck, filled with Genoese propaganda to the effect that all Corsicans, without exception, were little better than wild beasts, was completely won over by Giafferi's personal charm. Readily accepting the latter's proposals, he hurried to Vienna full of admiration for the Corsicans as a people and convinced of the justice of their cause. The armistice, however, was broken on Camillo Doria's orders, fighting raging again over the devastated land till in May 1732, the Prince of Wurtemburg, who had assumed command of the Austro-Genoese forces, received peremptory orders from the angry Austrian Emperor to cease hostilities immediately, and to draft a treaty compatible with 'the just aspirations of the islanders'. At the same time von Wachtendonck was appointed as an observer to see that the eventual treaty's terms were effectively put into practice.

There were strenuous objections from the Genoese. Defying Austria, Camillo Doria invited the Corsican leaders to a conference which was nothing but a trap. Luigi Giafferi, Ceccaldi, and Father Raffaelli, were seized, put on board a ship for Genoa, and there thrown into prison. It was undoubtedly the intention of the Genoese to have the men executed after a trial that would have been a mockery of justice, but by then, largely thanks to Wachtendonck's eloquence, the Corsican question had become internationalized.

News of the violation of the treaty caused widespread indignation. Wachtendonck and the Prince of Wurtemburg protested violently, accusing the Genoese Governor of deliberately insulting the Emperor. Other Corsican leaders, among them a certain Giacinto (Hyacinthe) Paoli, threatened recourse to arms to repair the injustice. The Duke of Marlborough's ally and co-victor of Blenheim, Prince Eugène, made a special journey to Vienna to beg the Emperor to intervene, while the Pope, Louis XV, and Philip V of Spain, sent their messengers with vigorous protests and demands for the prisoners' release, to the Doge. Obliged to climb down, the Genoese freed the three men, but insisted that they remain in exile, to which, rather than be cited as the cause of the breakdown of the truce, albeit uneasy, existing on the island, they agreed. Giafferi became a colonel in the service of Don Carlos, Philip V's son, while Father Rafaelli was given an appointment in the Vatican.

In 1733, involved in war with France over the Polish succession, the Austrian Emperor recalled all his troops still on garrison duty in Corsica. Their departure was the signal for Giacinto Paoli to lead an open revolt against the Genoese, and for Giafferi to come hurrying back from Parma. Re-assuming command, Giafferi defeated the Genoese in a pitched battle under the walls of Corte, once more forcing them back to their coastal fortresses.

Still feeling that Corsica was not strong enough to stand on her own, Giafferi sent a request to Philip V, asking him to incorporate the island in the Spanish Crown but the ailing Spanish monarch turned down the offer. Giafferi then decided on a unique step.

On 30 January 1735, a Consulta was called at which the Corsican leader declared the island to be an independent

Kingdom, placed under the protection of the Immaculate Conception. The Virgin Mary was the new kingdom's spiritual Queen, its national anthem the *Dio vi Salvi Regina*. At the same time, Giafferi Ceccaldi, and Giacinto Paoli, were nominated 'Primates of the Kingdom'.

As if overawed by this manifestation, the Genoese changed their tactics. Instead of throwing away still more men in costly battles, they shut themselves up more firmly than ever in their coastal citadels, and, exploiting their command of the sea, concentrated on maintaining a total blockade in the hope of eventually starving the islanders into submission. In this way they came near to achieving what their armies had failed to bring about. Deprived of supplies of arms and ammunition, of much needed food since war had rendered vast areas of their land barren, the Corsicans were at their last gasp, so that when two large vessels dropped anchor in a bay to the north of Calvi, and then proceeded to unload stores so desperately needed, the event was looked upon as a sure sign that their Queen, the Virgin, had indeed heard their prayers.

The two vessels, first practical evidence of British interest in the island, had been chartered and loaded by a group of liberal-minded British citizens, who had taken upon themselves to patronize the struggles of down-trodden races. It was a truly philanthropic attitude, but one which, Corsican historians note sadly, underwent a sudden change following on the later revolt of the American colonies.

In the meantime, it was again an English vessel, anchoring off Aleria, which brought to the island one of the most bizarre individuals ever to tread the stage not only of Corsican, but of world, history.

HIS MAJESTY KING THEODOR I

The arrival of this individual, expected by a few but kept a zealously guarded secret, was a total surprise to the islanders in general who stared in amazement at the appearance of the stranger as he stepped ashore surrounded by a small group of followers.

'His manner' says a contemporary 'was distinguished,

noble, really princely, his bearing grave and solemn, his costume flamboyant. He wore a long tunic of purple silk, Moroccan boots,a Spanish hat decorated with a magnificent plume; two finely chiselled pistols were thrust into the belt of his yellow silk waistcoat; at his side hung a sword in a glittering scabbard, and his right hand held a golden sceptre. Following respectfully in his train were eleven Italians, two French officers, and three Moroccans. His carriage was truly regal, and, indeed, it was his intention to declare himself King of Corsica.'

No sooner was he ashore than he was thronged by a crowd of excited locals, and if for them his presence was an agreeable surprise, they were even more excited by the cargo unloaded on his orders; 12 cannon, 4000 harquebuses, 700 sacks of wheat, cases of ammunition, and huge jars filled with North African gold and silver pieces.

This distinctly theatrical gentleman was in fact a native of Westphalia, Baron Theodor von Neuhoff – so often referred to erroneously as *de* Neuhoff – one of the strangest and most original characters of the century; for some a hero, noble, much misunderstood and sadly used both by fate and his fellow men; for others a common, swindling adventurer. In this it is interesting to note that the majority of his contemporaries, and those writing of him in the years immediately consequent to his death were, in the main, sympathetic, while the bulk of twentieth-century commentators dismiss him as a charlatan, a super con-man. Probably the truth lies somewhere between these two extremes: a schizophrenic megalomaniac, lost in his own fantasies, lacking the mental stability, the talent to crown his many ventures with success.

Born at Cologne on 25 August 1694, starting his career as one of the Duchess of Orleans' pages, drifting to the Spanish Court, then back to France, he next served for a time in the Bavarian army, dropped a military career to study alchemy, dabbled in politics, spent lavishly money he did not possess, earning for himself uncomfortable spells in debtors' prisons. 'He really was an extraordinary man' says another contemporary source 'He had seen everything, planned everything, tried everything; in a word his successes and failures cancelled each other out. He had made a fortune, lost it, lived the most incredible adventures, when suddenly his imagination was fired by the desire to wear a crown.'

This wild ambition at a time when the great powers were ruled by monarchies which had been established for centuries was probably engendered by chance meetings with the exiled patriots Giafferi and Ceccaldi. Taking an immediate and romantic interest in their stories of their country's sufferings and its burning desire for independence, it was not long before he was journeying round Europe, making friends and hatching mad plots with other exiled Corsicans. He then descended on the North African coast where his slick tongue, compelling personality and charm, gained him the confidence of a number of Greek and Jewish merchants and financiers, who agreed to provide the funds for the cargo which he eventually unloaded at Aleria.

Such indeed were his powers of persuasion, that he was able to convince the Corsican leaders that once he had been proclaimed officially King of Corsica, arms, munitions, food, even contingents of regular troops from sympathetic powers, would pour into the island to help his 'subjects' rid themselves of the Genoese.

There was a moment of universal euphoria. Certain that their 'Saviour' had come amongst them, the Corsicans had no doubt that when Neuhoff, calling himself Theodor Stefan von Neuhoff, Baron of Westphalia, Grandee of Spain, Lord of England (*sic*), Baron of the Holy Roman Empire, Prince of the Roman Throne, sent by God and the Holy Virgin to liberate Corsica from Genoese tyranny, was crowned King of Corsica on 14 April 1736, with a crown made of intertwined oak and laurel leaves, their centuries of tribulations were at an end.

It was not possible, however, to bluff the experienced Genoese for long. As weeks passed and there was no sign of the much advertized foreign aid, and reports from the mainland poured in to the effect that the 'King' was, in fact a bankrupt adventurer, plans were evolved to regain the initiative.

To forestall the counter offensive he knew to be inevitable, Theodor invested Bastia, then embarked on a lightning tour of the island to 'show the flag', and rally doubters. The royal banner, of Neuhoff's own design, was green and yellow and bearing the device *In te, Domini, speravi*. A royal coinage was also struck, the pieces being engraved on the one side with a crown resting on two laurel branches, and on the reverse, with the motto *Pro Bono et Libertate*. These coins were soon to be much sought after, not for their intrinsic value, but as collectors' pieces.

The root of the trouble was that having no money, King Theodor started off with an empty treasury, and even the most patriotic could not live on glory alone. Furthermore, like Gordon of Khartoum some years later, he had held out the promise of massive reinforcements, which he knew very well were unlikely to be forthcoming. It was not long, therefore, before doubts began to be voiced.

In an attempt to revive his flagging popularity, he paid a rapid visit to the Sartène area, creating at the same time a 'Royal Corsican Order' he entitled 'The Order of Deliverance'. It was significant that the Order's membership was not based entirely on merit. Always on the look-out for a little ready cash, one of the conditions of being nominated knight was the down payment of 1000 gold *écus*.

Disillusionment was growing fast concerning this first, and last, island king, and deciding that his gamble had failed and that discretion was indeed the better part of valour, von Neuhoff, no longer King Theodor, sailed from Aleria in early November, after addressing a manifesto to his 'people' and designating a further twenty-seven counts and marquises to act as district administrators. Needless to say, not one of those so designated ever took office.

Once on board, forgetting his crown, Neuhoff put on a monk's habit, and in this disguise landed at Livorno. Eventually he made his way to Holland where he hoped to raise money to equip an expeditionary force for the purpose of regaining his lost throne. However, far from finding support in Amsterdam, the city authorities, not in the least impressed to be dealing with an exiled monarch, arrested him for past shady deals, and threw him into a debtors' prison.

Despite their cruel disappointment, the Corsicans were not shaken in their determination to carry on the fight, returning so strongly to the attack that the Genoese, themselves exhausted and feeling their power to be on the wane, appealed to France. From their point of view this approach was a grave error. The proximity of Corsica to the French coast and its great naval base of Toulon, had long been a cause of anxiety, especially after the comings and goings of British vessels had created the fear that the English might be contemplating seizing the island for themselves. Delighted by this opportunity to intervene legally, Louis XV promised the despatch of an adequate expeditionary force to deal with the recalcitrant islanders.

On 8 February 1738, five French regiments, under the command of the Comte de Boissieux, landed in the neighbourhood of Bastia. With the possibility of eventually replacing the Genoese in the minds of Louis and his councillors, de Boissieux was under strict orders to try to come to terms and create a favourable impression with the 'natives'. Much to the chagrin of the Genoese, instead of taking the offensive, he issued invitations to the Corsican leaders to talk matters over. All seemed to be going well, when, unexpectedly, one of von Neuhoff's nephews, Frederic, arrived with supplies and the news that the 'King' was on his way at the head of the allied force he had always promised.

His announcement was based on fact. Having by some miracle talked his way out of prison and into the confidence of Dutch financiers, Theodor was actually en route, and shortly afterwards his fleet of three men-of-war and merchantmen, all flying the Dutch flag, dropped anchor off the coast. Though no troops disembarked, twenty-seven pieces of artillery, 1000 new pattern muskets, and 2000 grenades, were unloaded. But when Theodor himself stepped ashore, to his utter dismay, he was received with uncompromising hostility. During his absence, the Corsicans had had the occasion to think things over dispassionately. They saw clearly that they could not

7 OTA, typical mountain village
8 CALVI, the 'Always Faithful'

afford to indulge in fantasies. The brutal truth was that their King was considered a sick joke – or criminal – by all the mainland powers, and that any material aid he might be able to supply from time to time, in any case minimal, would in no way offset the disadvantage of being ruled, if only in name, by a man universally despised. All this the Corsican leaders made plain to the crestfallen Theodor who, denied by his Corsican 'subjects', on the point of being deserted by the disillusioned Dutch, and threatened by both Genoese and French, was obliged to turn his back with unkingly haste on his former realm.

In the meantime de Boissieux had drawn up a proposed treaty, but submitted it with an ultimatum that its terms must be agreed upon within fifteen days. The terms being unexpectedly harsh, it was rejected by the Corsicans, whereupon fighting broke out.

De Boissieux had expected that his regular army regiments would crush any resistance with little difficulty. Instead, after a five-day campaign which one writer has picturesquely termed 'The Corsican Vespers', the French were completely routed. Besieged with the remnants of his force in Bastia, de Boissieux was obliged to send a pressing call for reinforcements. These arrived, a formidable contingent of 50,000 men, under the command of the Marquis de Maillebois. This time it was the Corsicans who were overwhelmed.

The Marquis, however, had received the same instructions as his predecessor regarding his dealings with the islanders. There were no reprisals on the population, and though he insisted that the Corsican leaders take the sad road of exile, he refused to hand them over to the Genoese. Amongst those leaving their homeland, wondering if ever they would return, were Luigi Giafferi and Giacinto Paoli, the latter taking with him his younger son, Pasquale, destined to become an even greater figure in island history than Sampiero.

This second period of French occupation ended in 1741 with the outbreak of the war of the Austrian Succession. Every French soldier was urgently needed on the mainland, and again with the departure of de Maillebois, Corsicans and Genoese were soon at each other's throats.

The treaty with France being now nul and void, those exiled returned to the island. Fighting increased in savage intensity, and it was during these renewed hostilities there occurred one of those incidents so revealing of the Corsican mentality. The setting was the siege of Corte being directed by Giampetro Gaffori. By ill fortune Gaffori's son had been captured by the Genoese who did not hesitate to stand the boy on the ramparts, at the point where the Corsican bombardment was concentrated. Automatically, at the sight of the boy, the Corsican gunners ceased firing. There was a moment's stupefied silence before Gaffori was heard to order that the bombardment should recommence.

One is reminded of a similar situation during the siege of the Alcazar of Toledo by the Spanish Reds, but unlike the Spanish tragedy when the Nationalist garrison commander's refusal to surrender was followed by the brutal murder of his son, this incident had a happy ending. The rampart on which the boy had been placed, collapsed under the renewed bombardment and 'in the midst of its smoking ruins, there was the gallant youngster, safe and sound. Immediately the besiegers swarmed into the breach, and the heroic father had the joy of embracing his child who was unhurt; Providence had rewarded his exemplary devotion to duty'.

For the third time the Genoese appealed to France, and on the conclusion of the War of the Austrian Succession, another expeditionary force landed, this time led by the Marquis de Cursay, the French being more worried than ever before by further evidence of British interest in the island. In 1745, Bastia had been bombarded by a British squadron, and again in May 1748, a few months before the Treaty of Aix-la-Chapelle ended hostilities on the mainland.

From the beginning, de Cursay let it be known that he came as a friend not as an enemy. The Corsicans responded eagerly, seeing in him, as in de Maillebois, a shield against Genoese exactions. The Marquis's benevolent regime lasted for four years, till 1752, when he fell victim to Genoese intrigue.

Exasperated by his pro-Corsican attitude, the Genoese managed to build up a successful slander campaign – after having failed with an attempt at assassination – eventually managing to convince Louis XV that, eaten up by ambition, de Cursay was actually planning to have himself crowned King of Corsica. Backed by a wealth of false evidence, the accusations were so plausible that the Marquis was recalled, tried for high treason, and imprisoned in the old fort at Antibes.

As soon as de Cursay and French troops left the island, there was an instant uprising. The Corsicans determined never to allow the Genoese the precious initiative, were again led by Gaffori, proclaimed as 'Generalissimo and Protector of the Nation'. Though he had no basic military education, like so many of his compatriots, Gaffori proved himself a born leader, possessing an uncanny flair for 'a war of movement' and for singling out the weak spots in the enemy's defence. Soon he was master not only of the hinterland, but of most of the coastal fortresses as well. And once again, having been defeated in open combat, the Genoese were able to rid themselves of their enemy, by 'underhand' warfare.

The Governor, Grimaldi, was not mistaken in his belief that in Corsica it would always be possible to find someone whose hatred of a rival family would prove stronger than the ties of patriotism. Such a family was found on this occasion in the Romei, at daggers drawn with Gaffori over the question of land boundaries. The Romei brothers were, in fact, so obsessed by a pending lawsuit, that they were perfectly willing to undertake Gaffori's murder in return for the promise of a favourable judgment. Lured into an ambush, Gaffori was killed on 3 September 1753. The Romei brothers never lived to enjoy the fruits of the promised judgment. Together with Antonio, Francesco, Gaffori's own brother who, most uncharacteristically, had joined forces with the plotters, they were broken on the wheel, and the family home razed to the ground.

4 Corsica and France

THE MODERN PERICLES

When Giacinto Paoli went into exile, his choice of residence
fell on Naples where be became colonel of the King of the Two
Sicilies Corsican regiment. From the point of view of the
education of his younger son, Pasquale, the choice was a
happy one.

The city was noted as a centre of learning, its professors
respected all over Europe. One of them, a famous
politico-economist, Antonio Genovesi, was so impressed by
the youthful Pasquale's intellectual capacity that he took the
boy under his wing. By the time he was old enough to enter
the Neapolitan armed services – it was taken for granted that
every male Corsican must gain experience in the handling of
arms and the principles of war – he was not only extremely
well grounded in the trends of modern philosophy, economics,
and political science, but a brilliant classical scholar, and
speaking fluent French, German and English into the
bargain.

'His blond hair, with reddy tints, his blue eyes, his slender
figure, gave him a natural charm heightened by his
distinguished manner. His voice was clear and rich, his
manner of speaking fluent yet precise, his choice of words
inspired. Pious old Giacinto hoped that Pasquale would
embrace an ecclesiastical career. But his son had another
vocation.'

Beginning his military career as a *Primo Alfiere* (junior
lieutenant), he distinguished himself against the organized

58

groups of bandits terrorizing the country. His courage under fire was conspicuous, but 'like Descartes, Saint-Evremond, Vauvenargues and the young Bonaparte, as well as his sword, a number of good books were always within his reach'. He appeared well set on the ladder of promotion, when, at the age of twenty-nine, he received a letter from his elder brother, Clemente, asking him to return immediately to his homeland, to lead the country in its struggle against Genoa.

Though he had been in regular correspondence with his brother, the invitation was totally unexpected. The call ran contrary to his own, and his father's plans for his future. He was seized by fears that he was too young, had not the experience needed, to fill so vital a post. But there could be no question of defaulting, and on 29 April 1755, he disembarked at Aleria, at the exact spot which, nineteen years previously, had witnessed the grotesque arrival of von Neuhoff. Six weeks later, a *Consulta* proclaimed him 'General of the Nation and of the Immaculate Conception in her Kingdom of Corsica'.

The situation on the island at the time of his assuming power can only be described as chaotic; the difficulties and dangers confronting him enormous. The Genoese were preparing a major offensive to subdue the interior, while their blockade, re-established, was once more being felt. To make matters worse, law and order amongst the Corsicans themselves had completely broken down. Hatred between clans had reached such a frenzied pitch, that in their efforts to exterminate each other, upper-class Corsicans appeared to have forgotten the presence of a foreign enemy on their soil.

Pasquale saw quite plainly that his first task must be to stamp out the vendetta and unite the nation. Till this had been achieved any move against the Genoese was pre-doomed to failure. He acted quickly and ruthlessly. The killing of a fellow Corsican, instead of being accepted as a legitimate act in keeping with an antique code of honour, was decreed a crime for which there was only one punishment: death. No appeal would be entertained. Offenders were dealt with on the spot. A murderer who hoped to find safety in the maquis was vigorously pursued, and the chase not abandoned till the fugitive had been caught and was dangling from a noose. Paoli's law recognized no distinction either of class or family. When one of his own cousins took the law into his own hands, he was sent with equal despatch to the gallows.

Such Draconian methods, though welcomed by the great majority, roused the fury and bitter enmity of a number of the leading families who had come to look upon themselves as immune to the pursuits of justice, the vendetta as a 'privilege'. Within a few months, a member of the powerful Matra family, Mario Emmanuele, rebelled against the Paoli government. Raising a force of malcontents, he called a *Consulta* at which he declared himself to be the nation's leader.

Anxious to avoid civil war, Pasquale offered to put the question of leadership to popular vote. Matra, knowing perfectly well that any vote would inevitably go heavily against him, attacked. This act could have provided the Genoese with a golden opportunity to extend their own occupation while their enemies destroyed themselves in a series of bloody encounters from which the Paoli faction eventually emerged victorious. Instead, to begin with, they chose to sit back, hoping that this fratricidal struggle would so exhaust the Corsicans that they would be incapable of further resistance.

Though beaten, Emmanuele refused to give up. Blinded by hate, he renewed his appeals to the Genoese who, too late and still without enthusiasm put a small force at his disposal, and, early in 1756, led a surprise attack on the village of Bozio, where Pasquale was in camp with only a handful of men. It could have been the end of the Paolists. The monastery in which they were sheltering was set on fire. Pasquale, convinced that all was lost, had given a 'no surrender' order, when relief appeared in the shape of a flying column led by his elder brother, Clemente. In the ensuing struggle, Emmanuele Matra was killed, fighting like a tiger, leaving his rival undisputed leader and mourning that so brave and determined a man should have died so uselessly in protest against the very cause which should have united them.

The failure of Matra's attempt discouraged the tired

Genoese who broke off operations, falling back again to their coastal fortresses. This lull was welcomed by Paoli. Unlike his predecessors he did not look upon the war with the Genoese as the ultimate objective of his policy, but rather as a tiresome necessity to be carried to a successful conclusion before he could devote himself to the task on which he had set his heart; the development of his country into a sane, economically viable, autonomous entity, under a modern, democratic government based on the theories of Jean Jacques Rousseau and Montesquieu.

The Constitution he evolved in 1758 in the latter half of November, evoked the admiration of Rousseau himself. *'Il est encore en Europe'* wrote the author of *La Nouvelle Héloise* *'un pays capable de legislation, c'est L'île de Corse'.* It was indeed, from the democratic aspect, far ahead of any other government of the day.

Corsica remained in name a kingdom, but the monarch was a spiritual image, the Immaculate Conception, whereas as Jacques Gregori points out 'the actual sovereign was the people'. The governing body was a national *Consulta,* its seat at Corte, whose deputies were elected by popular vote. As an upper house, the general assembly elected a *Consiglio Supremo del Regno di Corsica,* at first of thirty, later of nine, members, not eligible unless they had reached the age of thirty-five. This body exercised the right of veto over the Assembly's decisions and also acted as the 'Supreme Counsel' with the right to choose the 'General of the Nation', who as well as being the head of the Government was also the commander of the armed forces, and head of the embryo *Corps Diplomatique.* As for the actual legislation, also largely Paoli's brain-child, it is interesting to note that some years later, another Corsican, Napoleon Bonaparte, adopted many of its principles for his famous *Code Civil.*

Pursuing his programme of economic recovery, Paoli concentrated his attention on agriculture. Acres were planted with chestnut trees; olive groves and vineyards extended, the marshes of the east coast drained. Parallel with this effort, disturbed by the low standard of education, he supervised the building of schools, and on 3 January 1765, presided at the opening of the island's first university, at Corte, staffed entirely by Corsican professors, and to which entry was free and without social distinction. This innovation was followed by the setting up of a printing press at Oletta, and the appearance of Corsica's first newspaper *Ragguagli dell'Isola di Corsica* (The Corsican News).

During this time, when more progress towards the people's well being was made in less than a decade than in the previous ten centuries, Paoli could never forget that the enemy, even though quiescent, still remained on Corsican soil, and still exercised a partial blockade. For a long time he had felt that being an island people, the sea should play a major role in the Corsicans' destiny. He remembered that in 1571, at the battle of Lepanto, it was a small squadron of four ships, led by Giacomo Negroni, famous Corsican sea captain, which had formed the spearhead of the Christian fleet in the decisive attack on the Turkish left. So, on his orders, the first purely Corsican navy was created; small to begin with, but with all ranks so imbued with enthusiasm, that it was able to break the Genoese blockade and inflict serious losses on Genoese shipping.

THE END OF GENOA

The Genoese, always realists, knew that their era as a power to be reckoned with in the councils of Europe was over, yet they could not bear to give up Corsica without some sort of struggle, hoping to be able to prolong their presence on the island with French backing. By what was known as the Second Treaty of Compiègne, France agreed to garrison Calvi, Ajaccio, Saint Florent, Bastia and Algojola for a period of four years, 1764–1768. But by 1768, after the Corsican navy had staged a brilliant combined operation, resulting in the capture of the island of Capraja, the Genoese, admitting final defeat, ceded the sovereignty of the island to France, the deal being ratified by the Treaty of Versailles signed on 15 May 1768.

Not only Paoli, but every Corsican was stunned when the

terms of this treaty became known. Without being consulted, they had been disposed of, sold like cattle. Paoli's words when he addressed the Assembly at Corte on 22 May, summed up the feelings of the whole nation.

'Never' he said 'has any people been submitted to so bloody an outrage. We do not know who to hate the most, those who sell us, or those who buy us. Let us mingle our hate since both treat us with equal contempt. I have been attacked because I have refused the terms of an humiliating peace. Before a brave and proud nation I accept this responsibility. I am proud to have done so. Do you know the fate that is reserved for us? The Marquis de Chauvelin (the French commander) threatens us before he has conquered us, dictates to us before the combat has decided whether we are to be slaves or free men. We still have our weapons in our hands, and yet he speaks as if he were our master. What would be his tone if we were already vanquished?'

Unanimously the Assembly voted for war. Paoli himself knew that they could never succeed. France was probably the greatest military power in Europe, if not in the world. What could a tiny people of less than quarter of a million do against such a colossus? De Chauvelin for his part was determined to crush the obstinate islanders once and for all. His first order of the day was reminiscent of Stefano Doria: 'In virtue of the powers accorded me by His Majesty, I have declared and declare, decreed and decree, as follows: every village or locality within the boundaries of the island of Corsica, which does not surrender to the troops of the King after being formally summoned so to do, will be sacked.'

Un Potentate cosi grande contro pochi poveri uomini (so great a power against a handful of poor men), lamented Paoli when the French armies launched a three-pronged offensive in late August. By the end of the month the whole of Cap Corse had been overrun, the French then fanning out south and west, confidently expecting all resistance to have been crushed well before the autumn rains set in. Instead, after a gruelling campaign lasting two months, culminating in a savage ten-hour battle at Borgo, which to everyone's astonishment ended in a severe defeat for the French, de Chauvelin, having lost 600 killed, 1000 wounded and 600 prisoners, was forced back to the shelter of Bastia and to call for fresh reinforcements.

England was now taking a keen interest in events on the island. A wave of sympathy for 'gallant little Corsica' being bullied by giant France, swept the country, and considerable satisfaction was felt when news of Borgo reached London. Lord Chatham, however, was not prepared to make a positive gesture on Corsica's behalf, and Pasquale Paoli, fully aware that however many victories he might win to begin with, his pathetically small army must in the long run be overwhelmed, offered to accept French rule, provided no Genoese were allowed to remain on the island.

The offer was turned down by Louis XV who insisted that failure to subdue a handful of armed peasants would be highly damaging to French military prestige. De Chauvelin was recalled, his place taken by the Comte de Vaux, who proceeded to build up his forces till he found himself at the head of the biggest army ever to operate on Corsican soil; forty-five infantry battalions, four cavalry regiments, and a massive artillery wing.

On 3 May, split into three army corps, the first commanded by General d'Arcambal, the second by de Vaux in person, the third by General de Marbeuf, the French took the offensive after de Vaux had issued another order of the day to the effect that 'the crops, the vines, and the olives of those who resisted' were to be destroyed.

Faced by this formidable military machine, the normally level-headed Paoli made a grave tactical error. Though he could only muster a total of 12,000 men, he also had under his command a small 'international brigade', composed of the purely adventurous mixed with the romantics for whom Corsican independence had become a *cause célèbre*, from England, Italy, and the German states. Their presence may have buoyed him up with the hope that massive aid was on its way, and that a repetition of the Borgo victory would decide those hesitating, but instead of withdrawing to the foothills where the broken terrain would have, to a certain extent, offset the vast numerical and technical superiority enjoyed by the French, he tried to halt their advance in open country.

After two days savage fighting, the Corsican line was broken, and Paoli forced to fall back to the Golo river. There, on 9 May, at Ponte Nuovo, the Corsicans were totally defeated. The tragedy was heightened when 2000 Corsicans who had rashly crossed the bridge to launch a counter attack, were forced back and caught in a murderous cross-fire. 'Four months later' wrote a French officer 'the bridge was still covered with congealed blood.'

For all time the fate of Corsican independence had been settled. The Genoese would never again exercise their sway, but, with the exception of a brief British interlude, the island was to stay French, eventually to become one with metropolitan France.

Pasquale Paoli escaped with a few stragglers to Corte, while his brother Clemente, in true Corsican tradition, took to the maquis with a band of seasoned veterans, swearing to carry on guerilla warfare to the death, rather than submit. A few diehards urged Pasquale to follow his brother's example, as Sampiero would have done. But the man who had raised his country from a medieval backwater to a budding modern state, could not tolerate the thought of its return to the jungle, and the agonies of a prolonged struggle whose end, in any case, was a foregone conclusion. Realising also that his continued presence might always be a source of latent rebellion, he came to the cruel decision that he and many of his more influential friends must imitate the example of their fathers and choose the path of voluntary exile, thus possible preserving some of the benefits of his 'reign'. On 11 June, he and a chosen group of loyal followers, rowed out to an English vessel anchored in the gulf of Porto Vecchio.

THE ANGLO-CORSICAN KINGDOM

Paoli was received with great sympathy wherever he went on the 'continent', and on arriving in London was entertained by George III, lionized by London Society, painted by Sir Joshua

Reynolds, and allotted a pension paid from the Civil List of
£1200 a year; a very handsome sum for the day. Despite
comfort, security, and comparative affluence, his dreams were
always of the 'liberation' of his country. He felt deeply
embittered by the way France had behaved, refusing their
offered amnesty in 1776, and it was not till July 1790, some
twenty years after his flight, that he again set foot on Corsican
soil.

During those twenty years, profound changes had taken
place. Though there was resistance by isolated bands in the
mountains, no national rebellions were staged as in the period
of Genoese occupation, and it was this comparative peace
which prompted the French to offer the amnesty in 1776,
already referred to. Nevertheless, to begin with, French rule
was harsh under the rule of the first two governors, General de
Marbeuf, who had commanded a corps at Ponte Nuovo, and
General de Narbonne. The possession of arms was a capital
offence, whether discovered on the person or hidden in the
home. Execution was immediate, without trial, followed by
destruction of the home and expulsion of the family. Bandit
groups were energetically hunted down and destroyed, while
punishments for comparatively minor offences were brutal in
the extreme. People were broken on the wheel, flogged to
death. Neither de Marbeuf, nor his successor had any liking
for the people it was their duty to administer, de Narbonne
even going as far as to put up a suggestion that all male
Corsicans should be deported either to mainland France or
the Americas, and the girls forced to marry 'continentals'.

Though the French were determined that there must be no
upsurge of nationalism, it was still their policy to win over the
islanders' willing co-operation. Parallel with his Draconian
repressions, Marbeuf was also introducing increasing local
autonomy, modelling local government on the French pattern.
When the country was made a *Pays d'Etat,* three Corsican
deputies, Monseigneur de Guernes (Bishop of Aleria), Cesar
Petriconi, and Bonaventura Benedetti, representing
respectively the clergy, the nobility, and the *tiers état*
(commoners), were invited to Paris and received at Court by

Louis XVI, while to put the nobility on an official footing *vis-à-vis* French peers, the King recognized twenty-seven families as noble, among them being that of the Bonapartes.

The head of the Bonaparte family, Charles, was one of the few Corsicans for whom de Marbeuf had any liking, despite the fact that he had been one of Paoli's closest friends. Descenᴊant of a mounted cross bowman, Francesco Buonaparte*, who had settled on the island at Ajaccio, in 1490, and whose son Gabriele had married a girl from a leading local family, Charles was convinced that the continuation of the fight was pure folly. Having the advantage of speaking perfect French, he offered his services to Marbeuf, not looking upon himself as a traitor, but as man of sound common sense, working for the good of his country. In turn, Marbeuf was so deeply impressed by Charles' intelligence, that a genuine friendship sprang up between them, the Governor unbending to the extent of agreeing to be godfather to Louis, future King of Holland and father of Napoleon III, and arranging for the second son, Napoleon, to enter the school for officers at Brienne.

This period of comparative calm was shattered by the outbreak of the French Revolution. To begin with a change of government in Paris did not seem to be of much concern to a Corsican mountain villager. How could so distant an upheaval, however great, affect his traditional way of life? The townspeople on the other hand suddenly remembered their dreams of independence. The New Order in Paris, they felt, should match their brave works with deeds and accord the liberty it had itself gained to all victims of the old régime's aggressive policies.

Serious anti-French riots broke out in most of the principal towns, but passions calmed when authority was given for the Corsicans to form their own national guard, and later, acting

---

* The question of 'Bonaparte', or 'Buonaparte', is complicated. The 'u' had been dropped in the sixteenth century, but when Charles, always a snob, discovered that he was distantly related to a noble Tuscan family of the name of Buonaparte, the 'u' was reinserted in his signature. It was again dropped by Napoleon as un-French.

on an impassioned pro-Corsican speech from Mirabeau, the ban on political exiles was lifted. In addition the pro-French party still remained strong, and included such influential personae as General Gaffori, son of the hero of the Genoese wars, and the Bonaparte family, Napoleon being back on the island as a young artillery officer, and it was thanks to their influence that, at the same time that the ban on political exiles was lifted, Corsica was voted by the Paris Assembly to be 'fully and permanently' integrated into the French nation.

Needless to say the now ageing Pasquale Paoli had been following developments closely, and as soon as news of these measures reached him, he decided to return.

Cheering crowds lined the streets of Lyon, Valence, Aix, and Toulon, from where he sailed.

His landing at Bastia on 17 July 1790, was the signal for a frenzied outburst of national rejoicing, and deafening cries of *'Evviva il Babbu della Patria'* ('long live the father of the country'). Yet despite all this, the homecoming was tinged with bitterness. He had fought and suffered for the cause of Corsican independence, never relinquishing the hope that he would live to see Corsica a free, truly independent nation, owing no allegiance to any outside power. However enlightened it might be, he could not in his heart tolerate a foreign tutelage, or accept foreign presence on his native land. No matter what measure of local autonomy might be enjoyed, his ultimate goal always has, and always would be, *de jure* central authority with every facet of Corsica's destiny in Corsican hands.

Though nominated a lieutenant-general in the French army and commander of Corsica, he could not reconcile his privileged position with his deep-rooted ambition. Worse still, as the French Revolution itself became ever more brutal and intolerant within itself, Paoli felt himself becoming more and more disillusioned and less prepared to obey the dictates of Paris. The time was approaching he felt, when he might strike one more, perhaps definite, blow for the sacred cause of Corsican freedom.

Matters came to a head when in October 1792 The French

Government having decided on an invasion of Sardinia, Paoli was ordered to mount a diversionary attack on the island of La Maddalena. The whole operation was a disaster. The French admiral in overall command, Truguet, was inefficient, his orders confused. Troops landed near Cagliari, mistook each other for the enemy, opened fire on each other, then panicked; Corsicans ordered to attack La Maddalena, mutinied and refused to disembark; a violent storm finally scattered the French fleet.

In Paris where the guillotine was working overtime, there was a demand for a scapegoat. Paoli seemed to be the perfect choice, suspected as he was of being a very lukewarm revolutionary. Marat declared him to be a 'cowardly intriguer', and to this accusation was added an official denunciation penned by Lucien Bonaparte. As a result, three members of the Convention were sent to investigate, arriving on the island 5 April 1793. On the 17th, one of the members, Saliceti, himself a Corsican, born in Paoli's home town of Morosaglia, informed the latter that he had been relieved of his command and replaced by General Casabianca.

Paoli refused to be liquidated. Backed by the vast majority of the population, he not only defied the Convention's representatives, but also turned on the French garrison. Casabianca was arrested, the young Lieutenant Bonaparte and his family were lucky to escape from the island; by the end of May the only strongholds remaining in French hands were Bastia, Calvi, and Saint Florent. On 28 May, a hastily assembled Consulta rejected French rule, proclaiming Paquale Paoli once more as 'Father of the Nation'. Fighting for her very existence on the 'continent', the only riposte of which the French were capable, was a decree proclaiming Paoli, and his ally Pozzo di Borgo, to be *hors-la-loi;* outlaws. On hearing of this in July, Paoli called on the English Mediterranean fleet, commanded by Admiral Hood, to help in the 'liberation' of the three centres still held by the French.

British aid did not materialize till January 1794 when Sir Gilbert Elliot, accompanied by two military advisers, landed at Ile Rousse on the western coast, their arrival probably hastened by the fact that in the previous month, December 1793, the port of Toulon, captured by Hood in the earlier part of the year, had been recaptured by the young Napoleon Bonaparte.

Though the three French garrisons were still firmly boxed up, Paoli was beginning to run desperately short of supplies. The British were welcomed as saviours. A squadron of the British fleet made its appearance, and in February, the first of the three French bastions, Saint Florent, fell. Bastia surrendered in May, and on 15 June, after lengthy negotiations, a national *Consulta* confirmed the break-away from France, the union of Corsica with Great Britain, with King George III adding the title of King of Corsica to his crown of England, Scotland and Ireland. Responding to the delirious popularity surrounding him, Sir Gilbert wrote 'There was never an act of the sort better sealed by the hearts of the people.'

In August, Calvi, obstinately defended by General Casabianca, surrendered after having been, mercilessly bombarded by the British fleet, commanded by a young captain Nelson, who lost an eye during the siege.

With the last of the enemy driven from her soil, Corsica should in theory have embarked on a sustained period of enlightened independence, yet almost from the first moments of its existence, the Anglo-Corsican alliance soured. As one French chronicler puts it sarcastically 'In twenty-eight months the English achieved what the French had failed to do in twenty-five years. They succeeded in convincing the Corsicans that if Paris were better than Genoa, she was also better than London.'

That this Anglo-Corsican experiment failed was largely due to the clash of personalities between two eminently worthy and honest men, who, however, were not armed with the mental equipment needed for mutual understanding; Pasquale Paoli and Sir Gilbert Elliot. Both furthermore approached this new-fledged alliance from totally different angles, so much so, that one feels that preliminary talks had been mishandled to the extent that neither fully understood

the other's interpretation of the documents they would be signing.

Paoli, and with him the entire island population, had never envisaged a simple exhange of British for French rule. He had imagined a Corsica enjoying complete autonomy, protected by Britain, the latter happy to extend this protection in exchange for nominal sovereignty and the use of the island as a naval base. Sir Gilbert on the other hand, was of the opinion that by the treaty of Corte, Corsica became an apanage of the British Crown, and as much subject to the authority of Westminster as Kent or Lancashire.

This divergence was accentuated when, to every Corsican's horror, it was announced officially that Sir Gilbert Elliot had been appointed Viceroy of Corsica, a post which Paoli had taken for granted would be his, especially as the Viceroy's powers were enormous. The Viceroy, in fact, fringed on filling the part of absolute monarch. 'Head of the executive and commander-in-chief of the armed forces (he) had a negative veto on all legislation, thus depriving the so-called Parliament of any real authority. The Viceroy could dissolve Parliament.' Though he was assisted by a Council of State, it was he who nominated its members.

Knowing that he had the backing of the people, Paoli determined to resist this affront – as he saw it – to the Corsican Nation, and blatant breach of faith. When Parliament met in the February of 1795, he was unanimously elected President. The outraged Sir Gilbert retaliated by stating that if Paoli did in fact become President, he, Sir Gilbert, would withdraw British forces from the island, thus leaving her to the mercy of the first invader; presumably the ousted French. The threat was too dangerous to be challenged. Increasingly resentful, deeply regretting having invited the British, Paoli installed himself in sulky semi-retirement in his native village of Morosaglia, yet deliberately fostering discontent which eventually led to anti-British demonstrations and rioting. At the same time, Sir Gilbert was inundated with petitions and harassed by delegations demanding Paoli's immediate recall to power.

12 Rural Corsica
13 `The church of Santa Lucia de Tallano

The Anglo-Corsican honeymoon was ended, Sir Gilbert, realised. In a despatch to England, he laid the blame for the poisoned relationship squarely on Paoli's shoulders, at the same time requesting George III either to accept his resignation, or take appropriate steps to get rid of the trouble-maker. As was only to be expected, the British monarch and Parliament sided with their Viceroy. Nevertheless not wishing to make the pill too bitter for either the Corsican people or their former leader to swallow, the elderly Paoli was 'invited' to return to England to 'honourable' and well-salaried retirement. Wearied by a life of struggle, realising too the strength of the pro-French party, Paoli – to most people's astonishment – agreed almost without protest to this velvet glove ultimatum. He sailed for England on 8 October, knowing that he would never see his beloved homeland again. There were no recriminations when he reached London. His retirement was indeed 'honourable'. He continued to be received at Court, and on his death, 5 February 1807, was buried in Westminster Abbey.

The British régime did not long survive his departure. There were fresh serious outbreaks, armed clashes, attempted uprisings which, though easily put down, still further embittered severely strained relations. By the early autumn, from the British point of view, the island was dangerously isolated. Napoleon Bonaparte, now a general, had just brought his first Italian campaign to a brilliant conclusion and troops of his victorious 'Army of Italy' were massing at Livorno, their probable objective Corsica. The fact that Spain was now allied with France made the situation all the more hazardous. Reluctantly the British government ordered the evacuation of the island, and, on 14 November Sir Gilbert and the last detachments of British troops sailed, the same day that the first French detachments landed on Cap Corse.

A DEPARTEMENT OF FRANCE

The greatest of all Corsicans who was to bestride the world of his day like a colossus, only spent six days on his homeland after his attainment of fame: 1-6 October 1800, on his way back to France after his abortive Egyptian adventure. As First Consul, then as Emperor, he dictated the island's fate from Paris, repressing all tendencies to traditional rebellion against authority with great severity, and in particular on the occasion of an extraordinary uprising staged by anti-republicans, whose aim was to hand the island over to Russia. Entrusted with the task of restoring order, Miot de Melito was told expressly by Napoleon that not a single guilty person should be spared, and that reprisals should extend to the rebels families, while de Melito's successor, General Morand, more tyrannical and ruthless than any of his Genoese predecessors, is always remembered by a reference in a letter written by one of his subordinates, General Cervoni: *'Le General Morand fait le bonheur de la Corse; on y fusille au moins un homme par jour.'* 'General Morand is determined to make Corsica happy: at least one man is shot every day' Yet understandably, Napoleon was always inclined to favour fellow countrymen who hitched their waggon to his star. Ordinary citizens who followed the Imperial Eagles became Princes, Marshals, Dukes, Counts; there were no less than forty-five Corsican generals in the *Grande Anmée.*

He may have been in many ways an absentee landlord, his paternalism that of the unbending disciplinarian, firm believer in the axiom that sparing the rod spoils the child, but it was he who gave the Corsicans a true sense of nationality stretching beyond the confines of their native *Pieve.* How could it have been otherwise when it was a Corsican, the Emperor of France, who for years had the monarchs of Europe trembling at his least frown? It was thanks to Napoleon that Corsicans began to look upon themselves as Frenchmen, indeed as super-Frenchmen, and when at the time of the Restoration, Corsica became a *Département* of France, for the majority this was but a natural step in the process of political evolution; many probably considered that, in fact, France was being absorbed by Corsica.

The last serious armed revolt against central authority occurred in 1815, after Waterloo, led by a young colonel, Barnardo Poli, husband of one of Napoleon's goddaughters, who refused to recognize the government of the Bourbons.

Though adopting a policy of terror, Louis XVIII's representative the Marquis de Rivière failed to overcome this last-ditch stand of Bonapartism. Defeated in a battle on the banks of the Orbo river, he was lucky to escape with his life, and after having been obliged to ford the river, arrived back at his headquarters both wigless and breechesless. The incident became a national joke. The Marquis was covered with ridicule, and Louis himself is said to have laughed uproariously at the thought of his pompous general sneaking back to camp, dripping wet and half naked. Years later, after Napoleon's death, Bertrand told Poli – 'you alone brought a few moments of happiness to the Emperor. He never tired of reading and re-reading the English bulletins about your war.'

De Rivière was dismissed, his place being taken by General Count Amédée de Willot, a brilliant diplomat, who was soon able to persuade Poli that his struggle was not only hopeless, but contrary to the interests of his country. A general amnesty was proclaimed, and celebrated by a solemn *Te Deum* sung in the seventeenth-century church of Saint Jean-Baptiste in Bastia, at which Polists and de Willot's men mingled happily.

It was not till the Second World War that this *Département de France* again knew the scourge of foreign invasion. After the collapse of the French army in 1940, Corsica remained French under the Vichy régime, till the allied invasion of North Africa in November 1942. The Germans marched into Pétain's mainland France, while on the 11 November, the Italians disembarked an army of occupation, which soon reached a total of 80,000 men, at Bastia. A movement called the *Front National* had already been installed on the island, and when a proclamation from Vichy was read to all French troops and island officials to the effect that 'the Marshal' requested that the axis troops be received *'avec correction et dignité'*, a counter manifesto by the *Front National* called on every able-bodied person to 'join in the fight against the invader of the homeland', and stating that its aim was 'to unite all those who prefer a life of continual struggle, if needs be to the death, rather than one of humiliation and degrading slavery'.

In its counter measures, the Italian secret police, the OVRA, and the Blackshirts, showed that they had nothing to learn in the art of torture from the Gestapo and the SS – 'nails torn out, arms broken, cigar burns, purges of mazout' – but despite the island's restricted surface, the mountains still provided the effective hide-outs that they had been in the days of Genoa. In January 1943, the head of the *Front National*, Fred Scamaroni, was landed from an English submarine. Shortly afterwards his wireless operator was arrested and under torture gave away the whole network. Picked up by the OVRA, Fred Scamaroni, fearing that he too would be unable to stand up to torture he knew to be inevitable, swallowed a poison pill. But in April of the same year another Corsican, Paul Colonna d'Istria, descendant of Vincentello, managed to get ashore and unite the scattered resistance groups into a single cohesive force.

In July, Mussolini was thrown out of office. The majority of the Italian troops were in favour of surrender, but from Sardinia 8000 Germans landed at Bonifacio. The situation became confused. Some Italians threw in their lot with Colonna d'Istria's patriot army, others, in particular the Blackshirts joined forces with the Germans despite the official announcement of Italy's surrender on 8 September. On the 9th, the patriots entered Ajaccio which thus became the first French town to be liberated from the Nazi yoke. There were still weeks of hard fighting before the island was rid of the last enemy soldier. From North Africa Free French forces were approaching Ajaccio. The Germans launched a counter attack, hoping to recapture the town, and oppose the landings. This was thrown back by Colonna D'Istria's, 'patriots' who also ambushed and destroyed a number of German supply columns plying between Bonifacio and Bastia.

Thanks to their efforts, General Martin's expeditionary force was able to land without loss. The final battle was for Bastia which the Germans defended desperately. It lasted five days, till 4 October, when the German survivors surrendered the badly battered city to Martin's truly mixed army of regulars from North Africa, including Moroccan *tabors* and *goums*, Colonna d'Istria's patriots, in whose ranks fought 'communists and curés, gendarmes and criminals, lawyers and shepherds', and troops of the Italian army commanded by a Colonel Gianni Cagnoni.

As Ajaccio had been the first town, so Corsica became the first *Départment* to celebrate its new found freedom. On the 5th, the following day, de Gaulle arrived to speak to the Corsicans in the Place du Diamant, by the equestrian statue of Napoleon and his brothers, in Ajaccio. After congratulating the Corsicans for preserving the spirit of Sampiero and Paoli and refusing the dictates of either Hitler or Vichy, the Free French leader spoke of a dawning era of peace and co-operation for the war-torn Mediterranean lands when *'une paix sincère rapprochera, depuis le Bosphore jusqu'aux Colonnes d'Hercule, des peuples à qui mille raisons aussi vieilles que l'Histoire commandent de se grouper afin de se compléter.* ('A sincere peace will bring together, from the Bosphorus to the Pillars of Hercules, those peoples to whom a thousand reasons, old as History, dictate that they should unite in order to fulfil their destiny.')

This Utopian dream has not been realised. It is true that Corsica has been spared the sanguinary upheavals that have ravaged North Africa, Greece, and the Middle East, but though the guns have been silent since the fall of Bastia, the island, like every other *Départment* of France, every other country of Europe, if not the world, is now called upon to face up to another great battle; that of economic survival.

5 The Island Scene and People

THE LANDSCAPE AND CLIMATE

I do not share the passion for islands inbred in so many natives of the British Isles, indeed three years in Cyprus are largely remembered for their claustrophobic impact. I certainly would not wish to live, even holiday, on those many islands which annually overflow with my compatriots. Yet I would happily live on Corsica, and love it as a holiday resort for the simple reason that it is more a slice of the continent, almost a continent in miniature, with its variation of scenery and its mountain mass which dominates the surrounding sea. The Mediterranean is simply present, not oppressively obtrusive; there for those who seek it, but not unavoidable.

This constant variety of landscape is all the more extraordinary considering that the island's surface is only 3378 square miles, that it is only 114 miles from the northern tip of Cap Corse to Bonifacio, and at its widest from east to west, a bare fifty-two miles. This means above all that the horizon is nowhere monotonous, that in a brief journey, measured in distance, there is the contrast of high mountains snowcapped for most of the year; dark, brooding, forests; what one might almost describe as jungles of chestnut trees which are unbelievably beautiful in spring blossom; shimmering olive groves, silvery when a light breeze stirs the leaves; gently sloping vineyards, and traditional 'golden' beaches. It means that even in mid-summer those who have had their fill of toasting on shadeless *plages,* are within an hour or so of the Alpine meadows dominated by such giants as

Monte Cinto and Monte Rotondo whose peaks soar to 9000 feet above sea level, where the air is fresh and exhilarating, but with that hint of chill on the upper slopes, as afternoon wears on, warning those not prepared for a cold night to make their way down to the lower slopes, before darkness finally descends.

Apart from the northern extremity of Cap Corse which is reminiscent of Cyprus's 'panhandle', the island has a remarkable uniformity of width from east to west, showing only an imperceptible narrowing in the southern region known as the Sartenais, after its principal town Sartène. The mountains running on a north-south axis, climb considerably more steeply from the west coast, and it is only on the east, from Bastia to Solenzaro, roughly sixty-two metric miles, that any real plain is to be found. Even this stretch is frequently broken up by thrusting foothills. This is the area that constitutes the heart of Corsica's rather shaky auto-economy; shaky despite belated efforts to modernize agriculture, introduce minor industries, and develop tourism after the manner of the mainland resorts or the Balearic islands.

These developments, and in particular the last named, while bringing in much-needed income in foreign currency and offering the possibility of local employment to offset massive emigration of the young, have not improved the landscape. Older generations can remember stretches of lonely shore where, they will tell you nostalgically 'you could bathe in the nude', which are now *lotissements,* or housing estates, and blocks of flats and modern hotels whose architecture is, to put it mildly, uninspired.

Though for the moment it would be an exaggeration to say that Corsica's east coast has become a concrete jungle like that of the Alpes Maritimes and the Costa Brava, much of the former charm has been irrevocably lost. Pessimists indeed foresee that well before the turn of the century, the traveller approaching Bastia across the Tyrrhenian sea, will be confronted with the same bleak, soulless grey mass that now mars the sea approach to Nice or Monte Carlo.

There is some comfort, however, in the fact that so much of

the island, by very reason of its tormented conformation, renders its exploitation at the hands of the planner barons, too costly for the rapid financial returns normally demanded.

In marked contrast with the coastal areas and immediate hinterland of both the French and Italian Rivieras, Corsica is a land of copses, woods and forests. The immensely tall 'laricio' pines of the great Aitone forest between Corte and Evisa, remind one more of Austria than any Provençal or Tuscan landscape, and even on the lower slopes where the typical Provençal ilex and cork oak flourish, they do so in far greater profusion than on the mainland. The hilly region known as the Castigniccia, takes its name from the veritable forest – possibly unique in the world – of chestnut trees which, till recent years, provided the islanders with their staple diet. As sea level is approached, olive groves and vineyards remind one of the saying that 'the vine and the olive tree are symbolic of the world's most ancient and beautiful civilizations'.

Unusual for an island is the very considerable number of rivers, short but incredibly lovely, among them the Golo, the Tavignano, and the Liamone. Most are what the Italians more aptly describe as *torrentes,* and because of the steepness of the path of their short journey from source to sea, they race down, water crystal clear, bounding in a series of cascades and deep limpid pools, perfect for bathing if one can stand the sharp shock of the sudden cold or near melted snow. The sight of a dried-up river bed is practically unknown.

Yet whatever the variations, the island scene is overshadowed by the mountains, always referred to as the Alps. For this reason the popular description 'A mountain in the sea' is so apt. What is fascinating is the nearness of the peaks! From the continental Mediterranean coast, one must travel a minimum of 100 miles before reaching a height of 8000 feet above sea level, but, as the crow flies, the majority of the island's highest summits are less than twenty miles from the beaches, with the strange result that changes of climate and flora are measured in sharp variations of altitude rather than long stretches of ground.

From the sands of the *plages* to 200 metres up, the classical

Mediterranean climate prevails. Most of the villages lie in the 'intermediary' zone from 200 to 900 metres where the chestnut trees flourish. Climbing to 1500 metres, the summers are still warm, but subject to short periods of rain, while the winters, invariably cold, may find the thinning habitations under snow from December to March. Above 1500 metres the scene is pure Alpine. Snow lies deep in winter, but with the thaw the white slopes become lush, flower-covered meadows, ideal grazing for the tough Corsican sheep.

Generally speaking, Corsica has a very well-favoured climate. There are contrasts but no extremes of heat or cold. The sun predominates but is never of a Saharan intensity; for the temperature to rise above 37°C (100°F) is rare. Though there can be cold, even frosty, days in the plains and all coastal areas, snow very seldom falls at sea level, and winter when compared with that of the British Isles, is mercifully short.

Official statistics for the low-lying regions most frequented by tourists quote average daytime temperatures in December and January as 14°C (57°F), rising to 16°C (61°F) in May, and reaching a peak of 23°C (73°F) in July and August, sometimes prolonged to September. The autumn is considerably warmer than spring, with October and even November recording higher temperatures than May.

Rainfall is sharply divided into two seasons, far more predictable than in northern climes. The major falls occur in October and November, with a lesser precipitation in March, while a rainless season that could be described as a drought, is an accepted feature of summer, but one that seldom has an adverse effect on cultivation since lack of rain is compensated by melting snows. This is not to say that there are no exceptions to the rule. As late as 16 May 1868, Edward Lear on a leisurely tour of the island noted 'Rain had fallen in torrents throughout the whole day, holding up only towards evening'. He had arrived in early April, and it was not till the end of May that he was able to write 'The morning is delightfully fine and the air exquisite' and 'Looking from the window, the red sunlight glancing on the thousands of pines stems of the forest, recalls the crimson light of the palms in many a Nile sunrise.'

The springing up of a sudden wind – a hazard in many Mediterranean countries – presents a danger to those out in small boats or even on li-los whilst in the dry summer months such a wind may threaten one of the island's greatest assets: its superb forests. From June to October, a carelessly discarded cigarette, a camper's fire, may start a blaze, which, fanned by a wind, has been known to advance at the terrifying speed of twenty miles an hour, devastating thousands of acres before it can be brought under control. This menace increases yearly as more and more tourists flock to the island, since no amount of warning, propaganda, pleas, or threats of prosecution, seems able to eradicate the 'lot of fuss about nothing' attitude, particularly of those from the north.

Officialdom is reacting. New methods of fire-fighting are being evolved, penalties increased; the individual who carelessly starts a blaze risks an exceedingly heavy fine, while the *pyromane,* the deliberate fire-raiser, may face a substantial term of imprisonment.

For the lover of the *plage,* I can affirm that the coastline is no exception to Corsica's prevailing mood of changing scene, and this throughout all its 600 miles. Most of the beaches of the east coast are qualified as safe, though on the west, in the neighbourhood of Calvi there is a superb *plage* for children and poor or even non-swimmers. Here a curve of sand of several miles slopes so gently that, according to the official guide book, the averagely tall person can wade out a quarter of a mile before the sea reaches shoulder level. On the other hand, round the *golfes* of the west coast, those of Ajaccio, Sagone, and Porto, rocks rise sheer from deep water, unpolluted, crystal clear, perfect for the strong swimmer, the skilful diver, the underwater fisherman.

Yet with all its beauty, Corsica is so much more than just an ideal holiday resort or refuge in the sun for the retired. Because of its tormented, heroic history, every inch of ground holds a story to be heard by all but the most insensitive. Few places on earth have such 'atmosphere', translating itself in the powerful individuality of the Corsican character. To spend any time on the island without attempting to share in this spiritual side of an otherwise comfortable, in many ways idyllic, existance, would be a sad waste.

THE CORSICANS

The first thing that any Corsican will say on being introduced to a stranger is usually *'Je suis Corse'*, this terse statement being delivered brusquely, and accompanied by a steely stare straight in the eyes, as if challenging one to dispute the fact, or, perhaps, make some facetious disparaging remark. The statement is, of course superfluous, for anyone with only the most rudimentary knowledge of France and the French, would hardly purport a person bearing the name of Andreani, Franceschi, or Micheletti, of hailing from Alsace or the Auvergne.

I remember so well the almost ferocious tone of this *'Je suis Corse'* when in my capacity as part-time critic for *Opera*, I called on the famous *tenore robusto,* José Luccioni, then Director of the Nice Opera, to ask for a ticket for a gala performance oı *Aida*. However, once I had assured Monsieur Luccioni that I was fully aware of his origin, that I loved Corsica and the Corsicans, adding that I realised that, but for its Corsican contingent the Paris Opera would have to close its doors, he was all smiles and charm, and I found myself not only with tickets for *Aida* but for *Lakmé* and *Rigoletto* as well.

The reason for this touchiness, albeit latent, is that even today, although one of the greatest Frenchmen was Corsican, and although ever since the days of the First Empire Corsicans have occupied the highest positions in France, especially in the armed services, the *gendarmerie,* and the legal profession, there still seems to be a shadowy ethnic barrier raised between the pure 'metropolitan' Frenchman of the mainland, and the island Corsican, the former clinging to a misguided sense of superiority above all cultural – much after the style of that professed in former days by the home-born British *vis-à-vis* the 'colonial' or the 'domiciled'.

To boost this, the mainlander loves to foster the picture of the Corsican as a figure of fun, the butt of snide jokes beloved

of *variétés* and TV comics. It has always been the habit of the
Parisian and the northerner to laugh at the Provençal as an
idler, an individual incapable of getting anything done,
spending his days sleeping under the shade of an olive tree,
quarrelling noisily but harmlessly over a game of *belote* to the
accompaniment of a glass of *pastis,* or, at his most energetic,
indulging in a game of *boules* in the evening cool of a
platane-shaded place. For such humourists the Corsican is an
ultra Provençal.

One popular joke tells of a Corsican settled in Paris who
had shed his endemic lethargy, was making a good living, and
invited his younger brother to join him. After lengthy family
conferences, and in view of the parlous state of the family
exchequer, the younger brother accepted, eventually arriving
somewhat disconsolately at the *Gare de Lyons,* not at all
impressed by the bustle, and shivering under a leaden sky. As
the two brothers stepped out into the street, the elder
suddenly sees an 100-franc note lying in the gutter. Grabbing
his brother by the arm, he points to it and says 'Look! What
did I tell you? The streets lined with gold! Go on. Pick it up.
You can keep it!' The younger brother shakes off the arm and
says indignantly: 'Now for God's sake be reasonable! Surely
you don't expect me to start working the minute I arrive'.

For some reason or other, 'lazy as a Corsican' is a label that
sticks. Yet after more years than I care to admit, and with my
acquaintance with so many Corsicans, met not only in Corsica
and mainland France, but in many far-spread corners of the
globe, I consider this stigma not merely an exaggeration, but
grossly untrue. If the Corsican does not normally share the
plodding nature of the nordic races, he is nevertheless capable,
especially when inspired by an ideal, of bursts of prolonged
energy together with an incandescent courage that mocks
both obstacles and danger, which few can equal and even
fewer surpass.

The Corsicans in the ranks of the CRS, the tough French riot
police, are those whom trouble-makers dread the most. In the
Foreign Legion many of the officers are Corsicans. In 1945,
Colonel Alessandri of the 5th Legion infantry regiment led a

fighting retreat from Cochin China to Yunnan, a distance of over 1000 miles, in the face of determined and continual Japanese attacks; a feat that has become legendary and frequently compared with that of Xenophon. In the days of the colonies, many of the officers of the *Affaires Indigènes,* men who lived in the heart of the Sahara administering zones often double the size of their homeland, were from *L'Isle de Beauté.* In 1934, it was calculated that 20 per cent of the Colonial Service, 6 per cent of the officers and 22 per cent of the NCOs and other ranks of the army, were Corsican. In the First World War, over 20,000 Corsicans sacrified their lives on the battlefield.

Like the Scots, they have always been great travellers seeking their fortunes far from home, and, sharing the heritage of most mountain people, have always displayed an inherent toughness, a capacity to rough it, together with a genius for improvisation, adopting the famous Legion motto of *Démerdes toi!* making them ideal pioneers.

Another reproach often heard, more serious, is that the Corsicans are a race of bandits, addicted to crimes of violence. This accusation tends to stick, for, as has been seen in the island's history, violence largely dominates the unfolding story. Even after Corsica had willingly accepted French tutelage and finally integration with France, thus putting an end to the centuries old struggle for independence from continuous foreign oppression, the vendetta continued, though to a somewhat lesser degree, and the bandit guilty of murder would take to the *maquis.*

It should be stressed that the direct translation of the French word *bandit,* as applied in Corsica, leads to a certain amount of misunderstanding in English. 'Bandit' automatically suggests the armed robber killing for purely material gain, a common robber who happens to be in possession of a knife or pistol, whereas 'outlaw' would be more appropriate, for on the island, the vast majority of those qualified as *bandits,* had killed, not for the sake of a purse, but for the sake of 'honour'. A seduction, a quarrel over possession of a parcel of land, could start a vendetta, a blood feud in which the whole family would feel itself involved, blood calling for blood, the whole *leit motiv* of existence summed up in one word; vengeance.

The fact that in the past the arm of the law was almost impotent, probably had much to do with taking the law into one's own hands. In a wild and naturally turbulent country like Corsica, people were not prepared to wait while the cautious, cumbersome and feeble machine ground into action; justice as a result became a personal rather than an official responsibility. Having thus vindicated personal – and family – honour, and automatically thereby becoming a criminal in the eyes of the law, the killer, or bandit, then took to the *maquis*, respected by friends and enemies alike, where in the tangled upland scrub living under the stars, life might be rough, but had the advantage of being practically immune from government retribution. Pasquale Paoli's ruthless suppression of the vendetta, it should be remembered, had been motivated by the national necessity of preventing members of the great families from slaughtering each other, rather than the foreign invader. Once a national enemy no longer existed, the vendetta was looked upon as a purely domestic, even intimate affair. Furthermore, from the beginning of the nineteenth century, the 'noble' families evolved rapidly, emerging from their feudalism, preferring to settle disputes across the conference table or established courts of law, leaving the villager to uphold the tradition of the classical vendetta.

The nineteenth century was in fact the golden age of the outlaws, who insisted on being known as *bandits d'honneur*. Often the description was apt, and officially recognized as such. Many bandits became international celebrities. They held court as if royalty in exile, receiving 'official' visitors, especially men of the literary world including Gustave Flaubert and Prosper Merimée. Flaubert seeing only the romantic aspect of the outlaw described one, a Laurelli, as 'purer and nobler than most of the respectable people in France'. Merimée's *Colomba* is possibly the best novel bearing on the vendetta so far written, as his *Carmen* is unique amongst the many gypsy romances, and particularly telling in that it is based on fact; a real life character, Colomba Bartoli. There may not have been 'women's lib' in early nineteenth-century Corsica, but as has been pointed out, Colomba was a woman 'of the traditional Corsican type, inexorable, single-minded, exquisitely cunning and possessed of an uncanny power to make men act according to her will'. Merimée, however, made one big concession to popular taste. The real Colomba was well over fifty, and not at all prepossessing in appearance. The novelist presents her as young and beautiful; but like any other writer Merimée had to think of sales.

It is hardly surprising that anyone in search of a good 'plot' is tempted by the current stories emanating from the outlaw society. One reads of a village mayor, Frattini, exchanging his *mairie* for the *maquis* after a murder, being offered an annuity of 1400 francs by his former *Commune;* of a certain Charles Camille Nicolai, killer of his brother's assassin, becoming the object of a female American tourist's passion; of the Bellacoscia brothers who not only denied authority all their lives, but even entertained those whose duty it should have been to end their exploits, notably a Prince Bonaparte, then *Préfet* of the island. When the last of the brothers died in 1897, his many admirers went as far as damming a river, burying him in the bed, then releasing the flood, by so doing ensuring that his last wish be obeyed 'that no man should walk over his grave'.

There are a number of other legendary figures. From 1820 to 1827, Theodore Poli styled himself 'King of the Mountains' after staging an impromptu *Consulta* of fellow bandits in the Aitone forest, and producing 'The Charter of Aitone' as his 'Constitution'. The Charter framed its own laws, and, as might be expected, paid particular attention to all details of 'The Treasury'. Taxes were rigorously imposed. Shepherds and tillers were exempt, but the bourgeoisie had to pay a basic levy of between ten and fifteen francs a month, solemnly collected by the 'King's' officials who, on receiving payment, scrupulously handed over a stamped and signed receipt. Even Poli's death was in keeping with tradition. A rejected mistress

led him into an ambush set by a special squad of anti-outlaw locals styling themselves the *'Voltigeurs Corses'*.

A few years later, the bandit Decius Viggiani, became so powerful, he was able to hold the city of Bonifacio to ransom, threatening a blockade unless a levy of 6000 francs were handed over, and imposing a form of curfew until the money was actually in his hands. The authorities were helpless. A few who ignored the curfew were shot down. There was nothing to do but pay up. Yet these same bandits could be sincere patriots to their comparatively new motherland. One of the Bellacoscias, Antonio, was certainly genuine when he offered to raise a corps of outlaw sharpshooters to fight against the Prussians in 1870. The offer was eagerly accepted by the island authorities, but angrily rejected by Paris.

It should not be imagined, however, that the bandit saga was all honour and romance; the other side of the picture should not be minimized, as one very factual writer, Felix Bertrand points out. He speaks of an informer having his eyes gouged out; of an outlaw mutilating his enemy, cutting off an arm, a leg, and an ear, then blinding him in one eye. In fact the mid-nineteenth century is referred to as *La Terreur Verte* (the Green Terror). In some outlaw-infested areas, people were terrified of leaving their homes. Windows were reduced to the dimensions of loopholes, gardens surrounded by massive walls. Fear of venturing into the open was so great that some installed indoor lavatories, unheard of at that time.

After the First World War the bandits began to lose their glamour for the simple reason that they tended to become bandits in the accepted sense of the word rather than *bandits d'honneur*. The new post-war race was making banditry a profession rather than a spiritual calling. Men like Spada – who nevertheless qualified himself as *'Au nom de Notre Seigneur Jésus-Christ, Spada André, bandit d'honneur et de vengeance!* his motto *Plutot cent mille fois la mort qu'une seule fois le déshonneur –* Bartoli and Romanetti, prefigured their Chicago counterparts, their motives purely commerical. Defying authority like their predecessors, like them also they entertained, but journalists, film magnates, rich and sexually-frustrated women, rather than princes and politicians as in the previous century. In the dawning age of publicity they gave exclusive interviews extolling the 'free life of the *maquis*', while indulging in the most brutal and sordid crimes. When the money they enjoyed spending so lavishly ran out, they resorted to gang methods of extortion. From being admired by villagers and bourgeoisie alike, they became first feared, then hated, as their image changed from that of Robin Hood to Al Capone. When at last Spada, most notorious and most violent of all, cold-bloodedly killed three men then burned their bodies, the mountain people rallied en masse to the police. A man hunt, unique in the Europe of this century, saw the outlaws, one by one, flushed from their hide-outs, most of them being shot down in the process. Spada was captured alive, tried, condemned to death, and guillotined on 21 June 1935. 'The morning of his execution Spada played a game of draughts, went to Mass, refused the traditional cigarette, the glass of rum, and the helping arms of the gaolers, and, a smile on his lips, walked unaided to the scaffold.'

The resurgence of violence, sequel to the Second World War, felt in Corsica as elsewhere, brought the bandit into still greater disrepute. Never for a moment after 1945 was there a question of reviving the suffix *d'honneur*. Outlaw activities were, and still are, confined to smuggling and above all to the vice trade, commonly known as *le milieu,* the word bandit synonymous with gangster, pimp, racketeer.

There is, however, this remarkable difference. In a world where violence, and in particular juvenile violence, is on the increase, Corsica is no longer an exception in that its murder rate constitutes an ever-present problem for the forces of law and order. If statistics can be believed, despite modern improvements in the instruments of slaughter available to any citizen, murder is on the decrease on the island but on the increase on the mainland.

What is noticeable, and far more so than in most other regions of western Europe, is the generation gap in spiritual matters. In the past, in spite of massive emigration of the young due to the lack of opportunity to satisfy youthful ambitions, however long he might be absent, however far his wandering footsteps might take him, however foreign or exotic his environment, the Corsican always remained fiercely Corsican. His goal was to return to his native town or village, his fortune made, to end his days in the traditional family and local atmosphere. Though contentedly accepting French nationality – since 1815 'nationalism' as such has never had the hold in Corsica that it exercises today in Scotland and Wales – *Je suis Corse,* is not so much a protest but a challenge, the average Corsican having no wish to embrace, or be associated with, 'foreign' morals.

Recent years, however, have witnessed a cultural revolution, leaving its mark particularly on the women. A girl was brought up to believe that the sole aim of her existence was matrimony and motherhood, the latter to be repeated as frequently as possible. Morals were of the strictest, pre-marital sex almost the equivalent of a death sentence, for any departure from the moral code was almost certain to end in the death of the girl or woman 'dishonoured' and her ravisher; classical beginning of many a vendetta.

Until very recent times a vendetta could be deliberately provoked by a gesture known as the *attacar.* To add to the drama, the *attacar* was usually performed outside the church as the congregation was leaving Mass. A man would walk up to a girl and either just touch her body or else, even greater shame, pull off her head scarf. As if a trained chorus – one is reminded of *Cavalleria Rusticana* – there would be shrieks of *disonorata;* the result, in a very few cases instant marriage, or in general the formal declaration of a vendetta.*

* It is suggested that the *attacar* is connected with an old Corsican form of bethrothal/marriage, independent of the Church, and mutually arranged by fathers of families. Dorothy Carrington, in her *Granite Island,* says 'the young couple met in the house of the girl's parents and there kissed each other in the presence of their assembled relatives. The girl's mother then handed the bride a plate of *fritelli* (fritters usually of chestnut flour); the bride offered it to the bridegroom, and following his example the rest of the company each

These standards were anachronistic, and though enduring longer than in any other region of western Europe, could not last. Two world wars, occupation, the influx of foreign troops, enemy and allied, followed by the development of tourism, the spread of cinema, radio and television, all contributed inexorably to the changing of the old order. As a result, the Corsican girl of this latter half of the twentieth-century is as liberated as any of her continental sisters, as free to earn an independent living, sit in a café, wear a mini skirt or bikini, as any *Parisienne*. And yet it is only fair to warn prospective Don Juans that a disrespectful approach is still liable to lead to serious trouble!

The question of language has also played a major rôle in this evolution. The island's true mother tongue is Corse, claimed by some to be a form of Tuscan *patois,* by purists, to derive from a pre-Latin idiom. Whatever the truth may be, it cannot be denied that Corse is extremely Italianate, the principal difference being that in most cases a final 'o' is pronounced 'u'. Before 1939, many Corsicans were tri-lingual: their own Corse, French spoken with a marked *accent du midi,* and Italian. Yet today Corse is a dying language, especially in the towns. Just as in Provence, fewer and fewer of the rising generation speak Provençal, Corse is now practically limited to the elderly and the mountain villages. The young speak only French. Italian is very much out of fashion, and if there is a second tongue, it is usually American English; and for the first time, quite recently, I met a Corsican in the *Corps Diplomatique* who did not like to be reminded of the fact that he was a compatriot of Sampiero, Pasquale Paoli, and the Emperor Napoleon. The revolt against the Italian idiom –

---

ate a *fritelle*, thus sealing the union by the ritual sharing of food. The marriage was consummated immediately afterwards in the girl's room. A religious, or civil ceremony followed, if at all, only after the birth of a child.'

Similar customs exist in Cyprus where an engagement often signifies the beginning of conjugal life, and a church marriage only takes place when the *'fiancée'* becomes pregnant. The breaking off of an engagement is normally referred to as 'divorce'.

probably due to the Italian war-time occupation – has led to a Corsican being as angry at being taken for an Italian, as a Georgian at being confused with a Russian, and a move to gallicise names which can be very confusing. Thus Cargese, becomes Karjayze, and Luccioni, instead of 'luchione', is now 'lucyoni'.

Despite this integration with what is still referred to as *'le continent'*, and subsequent spread of twentieth-century materialism, little has really changed in the national character. Though separated by only a few miles of sea, the Corsican and the Provençal, despite what many may affirm, have very little in common. Whereas the Provençal – the eternal Marius – is ebullient, can laugh, weep, fly into a harmless rage, over trifles, the Corsican is best described as 'dour'. Many visitors to the island comment on the fact that they do not smile readily, and can be easily offended. Spiritually, the Corsican can be compared with the Spaniard, in that he has a tendency to extol the idea of death, honour the spoken, as much if not more than the written, word, and be a stickler for etiquette; which brings one to the question posed by so many travelogues and treatises – 'How to get on with the Corsicans?'

The simple answer is, to observe the same basic politeness that is needed to get on with anyone, irrespective of race, colour, or creed; to be neither supercilious nor subservient. As for the Corsican in particular, it would do no harm to bear in mind that he does *not* appreciate Anglo-Saxon banter, often no better than ill-disguised rudeness, or earnest American criticism and observations on his institutions and 'way of life'. But one virtue the Corsican possesses to a rare degree, a virtue that makes his friendship a most precious gift: he has outstanding, unshakeable loyalty.

6   Art and Tourism

For anyone whose sole interest is the study of ancient Greece and Rome, or the greater architectural reminders of the Middle Ages, Corsica has little to offer at Filitosa, near Sollacaro dolmens and menhirs, dating from 3500 BC have been found, a collection unique in Europe. At Aleria, site of the original Greek colony and original Roman city of 278 BC, work on the restoration of the Roman city which, in its heyday boasted 20,000 inhabitants, is making steady progress, while in the museum, installed in the old Genoese fort, is a remarkable collection of Greek pottery.

It was during the Pisan period of occupation that the island was most richly endowed with ecclesiastical architecture. Many of the remote villages can take a pride in their little churches which are gems of Romanesque art, the most notable being Santa-Maria-Assunta of Figaniella. The Genoese, on the other hand, endowed the island with watch towers and fortresses, and although none could really compare with the works of Vauban, because of their natural setting the Genoese citadels, especially Bonifacio and Corte give an impression both of majesty and impregnability.

Because of the island's turbulent history, the *chateau* as opposed to the *chateau fort* is a rarity. Most interesting is a comparatively modern construction, the Chateau de la Punta, outside Ajaccio, built by Duke Pozzo di Borgo, constructed with material salvaged from the Tuileries after its destruction by fire by the *Communards* in 1871, and finally demolished on the order of the Third Republic.

Churches and cathedrals contain a number of beautiful

paintings of both French and Italian schools, many of them by still unknown artists. Ajaccio's Fesch Museum boasts one of the finest collections of the great Italians including Bellini and Botticelli, and of the Rimini school.

Though Corsicans may dislike being mistaken for Italians, they share with them a great love of music, especially opera. Throughout this century, Corsican tenors have dominated the Paris opera scene; Villabella, César Vezzari whose voice at its best always reminded me of Caruso, Romagnoli, Micheletti (possibly the finest Des Grieux of all time), José Luccioni, and most recent, Alain Vanzo. In lighter vein, Tino Rossi, who started his career in the early thirties maintaining his popularity on the *variétés* stage till well into the sixties, was the possessor of a unique tenor voice, warbling effortlessly with a curiously detached charm, his *J'attendrai, le Bateau des Isles* and *L'Ombre s'en fuit,* becoming world best-selling records. One may find today cafés, more aptly described as *boîtes de nuit,* providing music and song in the Tino Rossi style, designated *Au Son Des Guitares,* which most people take to be typically Corsican. In fact there was nothing traditionally Corsican about Tino's music in the way that *Flamenco* is so truly Spanish and *Wienerlied* so essentially Austrian. The *canzonettas* by French and Italian composers which made the cabaret singer are totally divorced from the real folkloric expression which, indeed, is seldom heard these days. Corsica has never produced a Puccini or a Massanet, and Vincent Scotto who wrote so many popular hits in the twenties, was not the Island bard, but rather France's Irving Berlin.

Improvisation, rather than formal composition, is the key to the island folklore which, so far, has not been exported. Corsica has still to find its Theodorakis. Yet despite improvisation, tradition is observed in these local elegiacs, as in Flamenco, mostly in a nostalgically oriental minor key, the form non-stylised, the length largely dependent on the singer's whim; the best known, perhaps, the *voceru paghiella,* and a form of vocal duel known as *chiama e rispondi.*

The *voceru,* always sung by women known as *voceratrici,* is an improvised song of mourning, usually for someone who has died a violent death, its main object to distort the facts to such a harrowing extent, that the living are goaded into exacting immediate vengeance. In the past, it could be said that the *voceratrici* were part and parcel of the vendetta. By-product of the *voceri*, the *ballate* are, as the word suggests, ballads, again improvised by women, in memory of a dead husband or child; gentle, melancholic, they express deep grief, recalling happy hours never to return. Most alive of the old song forms is the *paghiella*, exclusively for a trio of male voices, ideally tenor, baritone and bass, or three voice choirs, now a feature of sung Mass in village churches on the major feast days. *Chiama e rispondi* – 'question' (or more strictly 'call') 'and reply' – is a duet, exclusively male, in which the music is normally traditional but the words extempore, composed by the competing duo. There is no boundary for the subject which may be mournful or cheerful, comic, even farcical, or tragic, and as such may be said to be the only traditional island music to fall wholly into the entertainment category.

With such a colourful, action-packed history, it is strange that the best-known literary works on island life have come from the pens of 'foreigners'. As well as Merimée and Flaubert, Guy de Maupassant wrote *Une Vie*, the story of a honeymoon on the island, memorable for its poetic descriptions of the Corsican scene. The famous *Lettres de mon Moulin*, of Daudet contains a number of Corsican sketches, and the ebullient Dumas produced the lurid *Les Frères Corses*. Quite the finest work from an English writer is Boswell's *An Account of Corsica*, written after his visit to the island in 1765 during which time he travelled its length and breadth, and fell completely under the spell of Pasquale Paoli's charm, on his return to England laying the foundation of the Paoli cult which swept the country. Perhaps the two best-known local authors are Raoul Colonna de Cesari-Rocca, a very erudite historian who produced a detailed and most carefully documented *Histoire de la Corse* in 1916, a few years before his death; and the thriller writer Francis Carco – mostly stories dealing with the *milieu* – member of the *Academie Goncourt*, his better-known works being *Jésus la Caille,* and *L'Homme Traqué.*

It is rather sad that when only twenty years old, Napoleon began a history of his native land which he never had time to finish, entitled *Letters sur la Corse*.

'Let a landscape painter, having set out from Sartene, turn off the high road to his left' wrote Edward Lear 'there he will find on every side hundreds of foreground studies of incalculable value . . . enough work for months of artist-life', and he adds 'Since I made drawings at Mount Athos, in 1856, I have seen no heights so poetically wild, so good in form, and so covered with thick wood; and, altogether, as a wild mountain scene, this has few rivals.'

It does seem strange indeed that so lovely a country has not produced its own native artists to extol its beauty on canvas. But to the best of my belief, Corsica has never had its Cézanne, nor, apart from Lear, inspired a foreign visitor, as Provence inspired Van Gogh. If there is a future for landscape artists, surely it is here!

GASTRONOMY

The Michelin Guide lists, for gastronomical distinction, 12 three-star, 62 two-star, and 558 one-star restaurants in France. Out of this galaxy, only one Corsican restaurant finds a place – and that with a modest one star – *L'Auberge Chevallier*, whose *spécialités* include *pâté de merles* (blackbirds), and *poisson farci aux herbes du maquis* (fish stuffed with *maquis* herbs) at L'Ille Rousse, the town founded by Pasquale Paoli in 1758 as a rival to Calvi.

Despite this paucity, anyone liking strongly spiced dishes with the flavour of garlic predominating, will not be disappointed, provided that is, that the restaurant chef, or housewife, has not been infected by the *supermarché* virus. It is a melancholy fact that today, in so many houses and homes those lovingly prepared dishes which made France a gastronomic Utopia, are being replaced by frozen meats and poultry, frozen or tinned vegetables, and mass produced *pâtés* and *charcuterie* shipped over from the mainland.

To eat an imported mass-produced garlic sausage in Corsica verges on the criminal, for that made locally is unrivalled. I always found Corsican *charcuterie* more robust, more savoury, than that of mainland France or Italy, nor is there any lack of variety. *Salciccio,* peppery and highly-spiced sausage, is more meaty, less fatty, than most French mainland equivalents. *Prisuttu* the smoked ham, though not so delicate as that of Parma or Bayonne, is more juicy and a joy to eat cut thick rather than wafer thin. Other favourites *lonzu* (or *lonzo*), smoked fillet, and *coppa,* smoked shoulder of pork make the ideal picnic sandwich thick, crusty bread, liberally spread with mustard. *Figatelli,* a black sausage whose appearance is inclined to put off the finicky, and not to be confused with *boudin,* or blood sausage, is a blend of pigs' liver and mixed mountain herbs, and can be eaten either raw or cooked.

It is difficult to see why so many people object strongly to eating that *provençal* delicacy, *pâté de grives* (thrush pâté) when comparatively few send away that made from the other song bird, the *merle,* or blackbird. Whatever principles are involved, it cannot be denied that the *pâté* made from either of these songsters are delicious, and are usually served as one of the dishes of a good country *hors d'oeuvres*.

Corsican game is good and still comparatively plentiful, though, like wildlife everywhere, threatened by too many guns and easy means of transport. The *bécasse,* or woodcock, comparable to the fat birds found in Macedonia, is a delicacy especially when served on toast, undrawn and stuffed with *pâté de foie*. Corsican *sanglier,* wild boar, usually cooked with brandy and red wine, can compare favourably with the best pork. Partridge is a popular dish, but the birds are becoming increasingly rare not only as a result of the proliferation of local and visiting *Tartarins,* but also because of the gigantic forest and scrub fires of recent years which have laid waste such large areas of its favourite habitat.

Gastronomes claim that in France it would be possible to eat a different cheese each day of the year. This would not be possible in Corsica, though the island will probably prove a more rewarding hunting ground for the cheese lover than the British Isles. Most are made from goat's and ewe's milk, which lends them a rather exotic (or for some, objectionable) flavour, in any case considerably more individual than that of the ubiquitous 'cheddar'. The one which appeals most to tourists is *brocciu* usually served as an accompaniment to *polenta* fritters, as a sort of cheesecake known as *fiadone,* with fruit instead of cream, or, as one guide book suggests 'with sugar and local *eau de vie (marc* – a raw spirit made from arbutus berries)'. My own favourites are *Ponte-Leccia,* a blue cheese more like roquefort than gorgonzola, and a stronger goat variety, usually wrapped in chestnut leaves, and made in the higher villages where it is simply referred to as *fromage.*

It is only natural that fish should feature prominently on Corsican menus. It should be cheap, but it is one of the phenomena of recent years that fish, especially shell fish, is now looked upon as a luxury rather than a normal item of diet. It is lavishly and plentifully displayed in the markets, but the price is food for thought.

There is a wide choice – and I strongly disagree with the chauvinists who maintain that nothing that swims in the Mediterranean is worth eating – *loup de mer,* Mediterranean bass, *rouget,* red mullet, and *pageot* a delicious meaty fish with pink-tinged scales which makes an agreeable, and certainly cheaper, substitute for Dover sole. For anyone for whom expense is no object *langouste,* or cray fish are delicious. A favourite restaurant *specialité* is *bouillabaisse,* but this dish of a mixture of any fish available, once the staple diet of fishermen since it provides soup and solid flesh in one, has now become in Corsica, as anywhere else in the world, a luxury, for which one may pay the equivalent of not less than three, and anything up to five or six, pounds a head.

Trout from the *torrentes* are delicious, the fact that they seldom weigh as much as a pound no deterrent. Local brochures say that an expert fisherman may catch up to a hundred a day. If he did, it would be a great pity, because there is the growing danger that the best trout streams are being over fished. From the gourmets point of view, these trout should be eaten as soon as possible after being caught. Out of the deep freeze they are inclined to taste *fade,* the flesh limp and insipid.

Perhaps an acquired taste, but one well worth acquiring, is *oursin*, or sea urchin, very reasonably priced outside the tourist season. Half a dozen, or better still a dozen, make an excellent starter to a meal, and especially when washed down with a glass of chilled local *vin rosé*. A word of warning: get the *oursin* prepared for you. Doing so yourself is a long and tiring job, highly unrewarding, for lacking the professional touch one is likely to lose or spoil much of the small amount of edible matter each *oursin* contains, and at the same time collect a handful of its protective spikes, combination of a hedgehog's bristles and the fine needles of the cactus fruit.

Although eaten much less these days, the islander's staple diet was *polenta*, a flour made from chestnuts, usually coming to table as *fritelli* (fritters). In Italy and France where *polenta* is made from maize, it is one of the dullest ways of satisfying hunger imaginable, but prepared from the chestnuts of the Castigniccia, cooked in the old fashioned Corsican way so that it is succulent rather than mouth-drying, garnished with *figatelli*, and helped down with a powerful red wine, it is both appetising and cheap.

Like the general run of its *cuisine*, whilst Corsican wines may lack distinction they are most satisfying for anyone looking for 'body'. On the 'continent', the strength of the ordinary *vin du pays* is limited to 12 degrees of alcohol content – in the Perpignan area often as little as 9 degrees – whereas 12 degrees on the island is looked upon as a weak drink, fit for women (old style) and children. The normal draught wine in cafés is 13 or 14, and may even be as strong as 16. While stating that some of the wines he tasted were 'not unlike Burgundy' Lear complained that 'unlesss mixed with a large portion of water are too strong for ordinary use'. His views are not shared by most Corsicans, or present day visitors to the island, and the sight of someone adding water to wine is rare.

As in Provence, the most popular wine is the *rosé*, the perfect companion to a meal on a warm summer day, served chilled, but not as happens too often these days, iced; possibly the best is *Royal Corse*, named after the famous regiment. White wines are comparatively rare, and at times may be vinegary.

Personal experience is the only sure guide, but a dry white, Laetizia, a tribute to the indomitable matriarch, Madame Mére, will seldom disappoint. There remain the powerful, controversial reds, the universal drink of the villager. Even the best known, *Patrimonio, Fleur du Maquis, Mattei,* do have a certain roughness to the palate, but to compare them with red ink. is ungenerous in the extreme. They are a good accompaniment to highly spiced food, and certainly provide the proverbial kick for the tired traveller.

In the cities, especially amongst the young, the pre-meal glass of wine is frowned upon as being rather *paysan,* while beer drinking has become *snob*. Whisky is also very *snob,* but though the measures are usually in the neighbourhood of a treble, to be a whisky addict demands an excessively well-lined purse. I find the universal classical *apéritif* of the *Midi, pastis,* a form of *pernod* (or *absinthe*) with a strong aniseed flavour, turning milky when water is added, is totally adequate and very pleasant in summer. One can always find such *apéritifs* as Cinzano, Suze, Saint Raphael, and Cap Corse (not made in Corsica), or for the sweet tooth a local *muscat,* in the towns, but they are becoming less and less popular; there is probably far more Cinzano drunk in Bexhill than in Bastia. To all intents and purposes, as in mainland France, sherry is non-existent, and gin falls into the whisky price bracket.

Corsica produces two local liqueurs, or *digestifs; myrte* and *cédratine,* made from the myrtle found in the *maquis,* and the *cédratier,* a local lemon tree. Liqueur drinkers may find them interesting as an experiment, but will probably prefer to stick to *cognac*. Again for these inflationary days, there is always the local poor man's brandy, *marc,* often described euphemistically as *eau de vie,* a raw spirit made from the arbutus berry which, unpleasant to the average palate, could nevertheless restore life to the moribund.

One recommendation can be made – when in Corsica drink Corsican wines. Unless one's tastes are so refined that only a vintage *Côte du Rhone, Bourgogne,* or *Bordeaux,* is acceptable, to insist on a 'foreign' wine, and by this term I include those *vin ordinaires* from only just over the water such as *Côtes de Provence,* is a great extravagance, not even justified in most cases on the grounds of quality.

However, no matter what one is prepared to pay for the joys of the table, the present day traveller will never be able to sit down to meals like those which delighted Edward Lear, as for instance when at Sartène he was served a dinner of 'soup, trout, lobster, boiled beef and artichokes, stewed veal, mutton and olives, roast lamb and salad, butter etc', or 'Madame Pauline's breakfast of trout and beefsteak, beans and caper sauce, Irish stew, *broccio* etc, good in quality and profuse in quantity . . .'

TOURISM

More than those bent purely on culture, tourists or long term visitors who expect Ajaccio or Bastia to mirror the 'High Society' of Cannes or Monte Carlo, or Saint Tropez's trendy atmosphere, will be sadly disappointed. From such points of view, anywhere on the island must fall under that somewhat pejorative heading 'provincial'. Corsica is for those who prefer the quiet of a 'provincial' setting and atmosphere, to the hectic round of the 'right' places, of a modest one-star – or even starless – hotel, to those establishments guide books refer to as *palaces,* and to sip a glass of *pastis* or *gros rouge* served by a waiter in shirt sleeves or singlet, costing a reasonable price, than to drink the same drink, probably less generously poured, at double or treble the cost, crushed in some bar or overcrowded 'in' cafe terrace, merely to be in the vicinity of a pop star, or up-and-coming – or ageing – sex kitten.

If, however, neither the gastronomic nor the Society highlights are sought, I know of no better place for the yearly holiday whether it be one of weeks or, of a necessity limited to a few days. The *plage* lover has his sands, the more adventurous, the deep water of the gulfs and *calanques,* ideal for underwater fishing. There are shady walks in the foothills for the leisurely hiker; the call of the high peaks for the climber, a sport, or occupation, which becomes yearly more popular. Nightlife is unpretentious, found only in the larger centres, mostly of the traditional *Au Son de Guitares* variety, though the blaring disco now proliferates.

Nevertheless, despite emphasis on the quiet life, it cannot be said that Corsica is cheap. On the average, smaller establishments are dearer than on the 'continent'. But then the days of cheap holidays are gone, presumably for ever. There is still, however, one way of comforming with the budget, by camping, and this holiday form could be described as a Corsican *specialité*. One may camp either privately as an independent unit, or in one of the many 'clubs', such as the *Club Méditerranée,* the *Club des Amis de la Nature,* or the *Club Olympique.* Many ape a Polynesian style, lodging the campers in rush huts supposed to evoke a Tahitian ambience. Food is usually plain by French standards. Wine is sometimes thrown in for good measure, and at night there is the inevitable disco music. *Le camping* is indeed the answer for those with a family, for the young, and there are even arrangements for nudists. Each year the number of campers is increasing, and becoming more international, most of the sites these days towers of Babel, in which the distinctive Teutonic idiom tends to dominate.

In his book *Your Guide to Corsica,* Geoffrey Wagner sounds a very pertinent warning, and one which the authorities cannot afford to ignore. 'I envisage every beach in Corsica being in the lap of some *camping.* I hope it will be the right one.' He adds 'they seem to me to be systematically ruining some of the finest landscape in the world!'

From the native Corsican's view the situation is even more complex. That his island is still a comparative haven of peace in an overcrowded corner of Europe, agreeable as it makes the general tenor of life with its freedom from stress, paradoxically creates an economic problem threatening its continuity. For many years in fact, not only the islander, but the French government, has been pre-occupied by the 'Corsican Problem'.

It has its roots in emigration; the slow but steady depopulation which, first felt at the time of Sampiero and Genoese oppression, revived in the mid-nineteenth century when communications with the mainland improved rapidly and, as French citizens, the growth of overseas France offered ever more opportunities of adventure and fortune to the ambitious young Corsican, who, in any case, has always been infected by endemic wanderlust. The old song 'Farewell to the mountains, farewell to my home. My heart in the far world is yearning to roam', might well have been dedicated to the young generation of Corsicans who flocked over to the mainland, and thence to North and West Africa, to the Pacific Islands, and to the Far East. It was a population drain which was accentuated in the first half of the present century. In pre-war years Corsicans could be found in every rank or grade of all trades and professions, particularly in Algeria and Morocco.

The census showed that from 288,000 inhabitants in 1880, the population had dropped to 245,000 in 1901, falling to an estimated (unofficial) figure of 192,000 by 1962. As in Provence and Languedoc, rural communities suffered most from this drain, with the result that much potential arable land has been reclaimed by the *maquis*. This has had a snowballing effect on local economy. Till recent times, and despite its lack of manpower, the island had been self-supporting. All this has changed radically, and today even such products as wine and olive oil are massively imported.

Corsica must be one of the very few, if not the only, countries whose native population is inferior to the number of its sons living 'abroad'. Over 100,000 Corsicans, that is to say more than half the total of the island's inhabitants, live in Marseille alone.

It is a sad reflection, but a fact, that only the possibility of earning the same wages for similar hours obtainable on the mainland can lure the young Corsican back to his native heath or prevent him saying 'Farewell to my home'. The answer to this problem is industry, unfortunately for the lovers of nature, and though light industries are being implanted, industrialization is not being carried out on a scale large enough to call for a substantial injection of local manpower. The chief hope for the moment, much to the despair of the nostalgic, is tourism. Great advances have been made in this

17 Old quarter of BASTIA, threatened with demolition.

field in recent years, gathering momentum especially in the decade 1955-1965, and expanding like a vast bubble, as yet unpricked, in the following decade.

By 1970, there were over 300 hotels in the island, of which at least 200 are now classified in guide books such as the Michelin. Analysed, this means that there are roughly 7000 rooms to cope with the height of the summer season, but this is still insufficient to absorb the July-August invasion, though there is never the near chaos which occurs regularly at Saint Tropez where, in August alone, it is reckoned that in recent years 40,000 tourists battled for 3000 beds.

Tourism has provided a measure of local labour, but at a price. It is sad to compare Lear's descriptions of Bastia, Ajaccio, and Calvi, with the modern towns. In the haste to gain profits, planners and architects have sacrificed beauty for the functional, and the need to cram the maximum number of people in the minimum cubic space. There is nothing truly Corsican about these new concrete boxes which disfigure the landscape, any more than there is anything Spanish about the horrors ruining the coast between Malaga and Gibraltar, or Cypriot about the similar soulless structures which, prior to the Turkish invasion, had ruined Kyrenia.

What makes it even sadder is that the tourist boom has not gone far in alleviating the man drain. One reason is that the sort of work tourism involves, principally the staffing of hotels and restaurants, does not appeal to the Corsican who probably feels at heart that, rather than waiting, it is he who should be waited on.

APPROACHES

Today the journey from London to Nairobi takes roughly the same time as the journey from London to Marseille's *Gare Saint Charles* by rail and Channel steamer, and as the average package deal includes the air fare, most people who decide on a Corsican holiday, fly, undaunted by the fact that since there is no direct London to Corsica service, to reach Ajaccio or Bastia involves a change of planes at either Paris or Nice. It is a pity. Though including time wasted to and from airports

18 The ancient harbour of CENTURI (Cap Corse).

19 Genoese watch tower (Cap Corse)

and in changing aircraft, the journey is only a matter of a very few hours, and though on a clear day there may be spectacular panoramic glimpses of the Alps to while away the boredom of being propelled at a height which reduces the earth's surface to the proportions of a relief map, on arrival, the passenger has merely covered the distance from A to B; he has not travelled.

Unless in a desperate rush, to move south by train is far more rewarding. At least one sees something of the countryside, the changing scene as oak and elm merge out of the landscape to be replaced by olive groves, vineyards, and the umbrella pine, as sombre towns with grey suburbs are ousted by sun-bleached walled villages, and the passer-by doffs his raincoat for shirt sleeves. I know of few more satisfying experiences than to fall asleep after watching night descend on cloud-wrapped, rain-sodden landscape, then to wake with the sun bursting through the shutters of the *wagon-lit* (or *couchette*), and to look out on a sun-drenched earth, and up to the smiling azure of a Mediterranean sky.

If possible, it is best to use one's own car and not to travel to a fixed time schedule. Instead of taking the *autoroute,* or the main National 7 from Paris to Marseille and Nice, I strongly advise any traveller to spend one, or even two nights extra on the journey, and wander down through the wild Auvergne and Ardeche countryside, in the region of Avignon turning east through the Vaucluse and the *Haut Var;* by so doing he will have enjoyed a choice scenic *hors d'oeuvres* to the Corsican main dish.

Depending on whether you like a longish or short sea crossing, the choice of embarkation from the mainland lies between Marseille or Nice to Ajaccio and Bastia, by the comfortable boats of the Compagnie Générale Trans-Méditérranéenne, in the *Corse,* the *Napoléon,* the *F. Scaramoni* (named after the Corsican resistance leader who committed suicide fearing that he might break down under torture and reveal the secrets of the network), and the *Roussillon.* It is a ten to 12-hour voyage from Marseille, about five to six hours from Nice, the accommodation of the 'ferry' varieity, a ticket entitling the passenger to his share of deck space with cabins and food extra. There is a less-popular service from Nice to L'Ile Rousse, and at the peak of the tourist season sailings from Toulon, some of the boats on this latter service calling at Propriano, a small port on the south-west coast, at the head of the gulf of Valinco.

Sailings are frequent, varying from twenty a week on the Trans-Méditérranéenne from July to mid-September, to twenty-five a month in the off season. In addition, anyone wishing to vary their Corsican stay can make a short visit to Italy or Sardinia by the Italian Line Tirrenia, or the Corsican Compagnie de Navigation.

The normal flight time from Paris to Bastia or Ajaccio is one hour and forty minutes.

7   Ajaccio: the Imperial City

Ajaccio, c'est le souvenir de Napoléon avec des maisons autour.

The British tend to complain that foreign resorts are dirty; 'Smell Naples and die' has become a classical phrase worthy of a place in the *Penguin Dictionary of Modern Quotations*. However when applied to Ajaccio, and to a lesser extent the town of Grasse in the Alpes Maritimes, 'smell' becomes 'scent' the qualification bestowed as the highest of all praises. For instance – 'It was there that we caught the scent of the *maquis,* borne out on a warm land breeze. This is the scent of all Corsica; bitter sweet, akin to incense, heady almost, as an anaesthetic after rain.'

The author is writing about her approach to Ajaccio from the sea, and though unable to claim so sensitive a nose, for me, the visual beauty of the scene more than compensates for any lack of olfactory appreciation. Indeed, if one is to make comparisons, the Bay of Ajaccio is infinitely more beautiful than the more famous Bay of Naples.

The town is spread out along the northern shore of the Golfe d'Ajaccio, sweetened by the waters of the Prunelli river which cascade down from Monte Renoso, and framed by the mass of Monte d'Oro, one of the island's highest peaks. From a distance one has the impression of a tight white phalanx of buildings crowned by the universal red of Provençal tiles, and it is only as the distance to shore lessens that one becomes aware of the ugly rectilineal blocks of modern buildings acting as a barrier to the land side. Yet even this cannot spoil the setting; that outer ring of Alpine-like peaks, the dark purple of distant forests, the heavy spread of the *maquis,* and the sheen of olive groves when, in a light breeze, the leaves of the trees resemble fine-spun silver thread.

As a city Ajaccio may not be distinguished for its architectural splendours or art treasures, but even so it does not merit Lear's reproaches: 'No charm either of colour or architecture in public or other buildings salute the eye . . . no wealth of tall campanile or graceful spire.' The streets and squares are dignified, pleasantly lined by palms, more prolific on the island than the mainland, and the ubiquitous *platane,* while there is no lack of the picturesque in the many back alleys off the main thoroughfares, narrow, arched, lined by immensely tall houses, each one in itself a potential fortress.

The original Ajaccio was destroyed by the Saracens in the tenth century, then rebuilt by the Genoese some two kilometres to the north of the present emplacement. But it was not till the island was taken over by the bank of Saint George (handed over by Genoa in 1453) that it began to develop as a city of major importance. Rather like a cantonment in British India or a *ville nouvelle* of French Morocco, the Bank intended to make the 'modern' Ajaccio a centre reserved for the occupiers to the exclusion of the natives. Not indeed till the Napoleonic era did Ajaccio come to rival, and eventually surpass, Bastis, Calvi and Corte.

It was the Convention which in 1793 divided the island into two *Départements,* to be known as Golo and Liamone, Ajaccio being decreed the *chef lieu* of the latter. Finally on 19 April 1811 the two *Départements* were united, and the reigning Emperor's birthplace named as the capital.

To begin with, therefore, Ajaccio is a must for the many millions who today, more than 200 years after his birth, are still fascinated by the life and legend of *L'Empereur,* the five foot two giant who, for so many years, held the destiny of continental Europe in the hollow of his hand. Though once he had attained power, Napoleon neglected his home land, his influence on the psychological aspect of Franco-Corsican relations was of supreme importance. It has been seen how, for well over 1000 years, succeeding generations of Corsicans had fought and died in the struggle to throw off foreign domination, including since 1739, that of France. But when a native born of a well-established Corsican family became Emperor of the French, the whole attitude changed. It was true that Paris remained France's capital; but an islander dictated his will to Paris. From that moment, far from feeling that their precious independence was lost, the Corsicans came to look on themselves not merely as Frenchmen, but as super-Frenchmen, the *Herrenvolk* of the French nation.

Ajaccio's many memorials to this greatest of all Corsicans are surprisingly modest, but of real interest, permeated with sincerity. The first visit of this Napoleonic tour should be to the very beginning of the legend, the house in which he was born; the Casa, or as it is usually called these days, the Maison Bonaparte in the Rue Saint Charles, a solid, three-storey house, built in the early seventeenth century.

Napoleon saw the light of day on 15 August the year of the Corsican disaster at Ponte Nuovo, a disaster which persuaded his father Carlo, that from then on he would be Charles – *'J'ai été'* he is reported have said *'bon patriote et Paoliste dans l'âme tant qu'a duré le gouvernement national, mais ce gouvernement n'est plus. Nous voila Francais.'* 'I have been a good patriot and Paolist at heart so long as the national government existed, but it exists no longer. So let us all be French!' This change of heart paid dividends. In 1771, Charles was chosen as a member of the *Commission des Douze Nobles,* and six years later elected as the deputy of the Corsican nobility to act as the island's representative at Versailles. His wife Laetitia – the future Madame Mère – was also a woman of property, so that the suggestion that the Emperor Napoleon was of humble indigent parentage is pure myth. Charles died in February 1785, by which time, thanks to French patronage, most of his children seemed to have a safe future carved for them.

When the Bonaparte family had to quit the island in a hurry to escape from the temporarily triumphant Poalists and the English, the Maison Bonaparte was requisitioned by the latter as an officers' billet, one of the officers lodged there being a young ensign named Hudson Lowe. On her return, after the departure of the English, in 1798, Madame Mère was given a grant of 97,500 francs as compensation for the damage done to her property during its occupation, money which she spent mostly on purchasing the furniture now on show. In 1804, Napoleon made a gift of the house to his mother's cousin, Andrea Remolino, who in turn left it in his will to Joseph, King of Spain. The last Bonaparte to own the property was Prince Victor, descendant of Jerome, Benjamin of the family, and once King of Westphalia, who in turn donated it to the French nation in 1923.

On the first floor, mainly taken up by Madame Mère's salon, there is the display of the *Directoire* furniture bought after receiving the grant already mentioned, more of interest for its association than for its particular merit as furniture. In the bedroom, rather inevitably, there is a Louis XV bed, in which the Bonapartes spent their wedding night, and in which most of their *famille nombreuse* were born. There is a general air of wealthy gentility about this establishment, though by contrast the almost monastic simplicity of Napoleon's bedroom, with its unadorned white walls seems to be a foretaste of the future Emperor's preference for a camp bed. In this room is the trap door under a cupboard in one corner, by which he was able to slip down to the ground floor, and thence make his escape to the Rue Notre-Dame. There are, however, two versions, utterly contradictory, as to why this trap door was used. The more dramatic suggests that it was to escape from the Paolists, the other that it was to avoid the embarrassing enthusiasm of his admirers on his return from Egypt in 1799!

The Musée Napoléonien is on the north side of the Place Marechal Foch, close to the Gare Maritime, and forming the angle with the Quai Napoleon. It is housed on the first floor of the Hotel de Ville, built in 1826 during the reign of Charles X, and whose ground floor is occupied by the tourist office, the *Syndicat d'Initiative*. This Napoleonic Museum has a unique collection of busts and portraits of the Imperial family by the best-known portraitists of the day. My favourites are Gérard's portrait of Joseph in his robes as King of Spain, one of the rare portraits of Charles (Carlo) Bonaparte by Girodet, and the charmingly frilly Winterhalter of Napoleon III and the Empress Eugénie. There is the interesting baptismal act of Napoleon which, dated 21 July 1771, shows that he was not baptised till he was 23 months old, and signed by 'J. B. Diamante, *curé* – Laurent Giubega – Geltruda Paravicino – Charles Bonaparte,' and, not to be missed, the collection of medals, decorations, and coins, laid out in a small neighbouring room, covering the period 1797 to 1876, a gift of Prince Napoleon, better known as Plon-Plon.

Tragic, by reason of its association, is the bust, by Bosio, of the infant King of Rome, Napoleon's son by his second wife, the Austrian Marie-Louise, which accompanied him to occupy the place of honour in his bedroom at Saint Helena. This can be seen on the mantelpiece, and – final memory – the Emperor's bronze death mask, pathetically youthful in its tranquillity, as though death had suddenly rejuvenated the sad exile.

From the western end of the Place Maréchal Foch, the Rue Cardinal Fesch leads to the Chapelle Impériale and the Musée Fesch.

The chapel built in 1855 on the orders of Napoleon III, is another of Prince Victor's gifts to the nation. This cruciform building is the work of Jerome Maglioli, a Corsican who was both painter and architect. Here rest nine Bonapartes and the tombs of seven, including Napoleon's father and mother and of Cardinal Fesch himself, are to be seen in the crypt while that of Prince Victor, the donator, and his wife Clementine, are above the stairway. The others are those of the children and grandchildren of Lucien, least famous of the imperial family, ferocious republican and opponent of Paoli. His theories on equality were diverse. They did not prevent him making a vast personal fortune, but when his brother, dropping the title of First Consul assumed that of Emperor, he retired from public life in protest. In 1810, he attempted to reach republican America, but his ship was intercepted by a British frigate. As a result he spent the years till 1814 as a semi-prisoner. Like Louis, ex-King of Holland, he retired to

Italy after the Hundred Days, dying there in 1840.

The Musée Fesch cannot be missed by a lover of early Italian painting. (Admittance is covered by the ticket bought for the Musée Napoléonien.) The splendid collection it houses owes its existence to the magpie instincts of Napoleon's step-uncle, Cardinal Fesch, son of Napoleon's maternal grandmother and a Swiss officer in the Genoese army. Like Reichsmarschall Goering some 150 years later, he took advantage of the fact that cities guarding the world's greatest art treasures were being overrun by his country's armies, to amass an impressive hoard of canvases of the fourteenth and fifteenth-century Italian schools.

After the restoration, Fesch, who had become Archbishop of Lyons in 1802, Cardinal in 1803, and finally *Grand Aumonier de L'Empire, Comte et Senateur,* hoped to be allowed to retain his position of Archbishop by offering his great collection to the nation. This, however, the Bourbon monarch was not prepared to allow. Fesch then had the idea of building an Academy at Ajaccio to which he would bequeath the choicest pieces in his possession. He died before the Academy was properly installed, thus giving time for his legatee, Joseph Bonaparte to oppose the will and insist that he, Joseph, should decide which of the canvases should adorn the Academy's walls. Fortunately Joseph, who was no connoisseur, retained the more modern works, which he preferred, so that those we see today are the very pick of the original collection.

The Museum, which is due to be considerably enlarged, houses some 1,200 canvases and can be visited every day of the week, including Sundays in the summer months. It is not the purpose of this book to serve as a catalogue of these treasures, but I would suggest that rather than spend an hour or two as some guides advise, a whole day is needed for a full appreciation. Of the earlier works, showing the first breakaway from the highly-stylised Byzantine formulae, my favourite is a Last Judgment of the Florentine school, whose greatest exponent was, perhaps, Giotto. In the room devoted to the fifteenth century, there is a superb painting of the Virgin by Sandro Botticelli, probably finished in 1470, and a

Madone et Les Deux Saints by Cosimo Tura, of the Ferrari school. In the sixteenth-century hall, one should not miss Titian's (Vecelli Tiziano) 'Second Man with a Glove' – the 'First' is in the Louvre – or Veronese's (Paolo Cagliari) 'Leda', and later, for those who like a picture postcard, but nevertheless highly attractive, form of art, there are the works of the two Canalettos, uncle and nephew. If I had to pick my favourite, it would be the Botticelli.

Below the museum, on the ground floor, is the Library, actually founded by Lucien (Bonaparte) when Minister of the Interior in 1800, and which now claims to shelter some 50,000 volumes.

The Cathedral dates back to 1554, work of Giacomo della Porta, architect of Pope Gregory XIII, and was not completed till 1593. There is a magnificent Delacroix, *Vierge du Sacre Coeur*, in the first chapel to the left, built by Pietro-Paolo d'Ornano to the memory of his only son, and decorated with stuccos which, it is suggested, are the work of Tintoretto, but the Cathedral itself today serves rather as yet another reminder of the Emperor. The superb white marble High Altar, was a gift of Napoleon's sister, Elisa Bacciocchi, while to the right of the main entrance is the white marble font which was used on the occasion of his baptism. In the second chapel to the right is a medallion offered by Madame Mère as a thanksgiving for her son's first great victory at Montenotte; to the left a plaque commemorating Napoleon's words a few days before his death in May 1821 – '*Si on proscrit mon cadavre comme on a proscrit ma personne, je souhaite qu'on m'inhume auprès de mes ancetres dans la Cathédrale d'Ajaccio en Corse.*'(If my dead body is proscribed as my living person has been, I would wish to be buried beside my forbears in the Cathedral of Ajaccio in Corsica.)

In the city's streets, three statues, none of them very impressive, ensure that one does not forget that this is indeed the 'Imperial' city. Largest and most ambitious is to be found on the principal square, the Place General de Gaulle, prior to 1945 the Place du Diamant. Based on a design by Viollet-le-Duc, restorer of Avignon's ramparts, it represents

Napoleon on horseback in the robes of a Roman Emperor, framed by his four brothers in togas. Personally, I have never been able to understand the habit of clothing contemporary figures in the habits of ancient Rome; far from bestowing an Imperial aura, even in stone or bronze, the subjects always look slightly ridiculous, as if they had been caught out returning from a fancy-dress ball. The same can be said of the statue of Napoleon on the Place du Marechal Foch, where accompanied by four lions instead of four brothers, Napoleon is shown as First Consul, this time himself wearing a toga. The ensemble is the joint work of the Corsican Maglioli, responsible for the lions, and of the Frenchman, Laboureur, who sculpted the First Consul.

More interesting here is the little statute of the Virgin Mary – La Madonuccia, or Notre Dame de Miséricorde – placed in a niche of a neighbouring house, with its inscription on the plinth *Posuerunt me custodem* (they placed me as guardian). It was in 1656, when the dreaded black plague was devastating Genoa itself, that the people of Ajaccio consecrated their city to Our Lady of Mercy, in the hope that Her protection would spare them the horrors of an epidemic. Their prayers were answered; the plague passed them by, since when the *Fête de la Miséricorde,* 18 March, has been one of the great church festivals of the year. This miracle was further recorded in 1739, when the second chapel on the left in the Cathedral was built at public expense, and dedicated to La Madonuccia, one of the three frescoes depicting 'Ajaccio saved from the Plague by an Angel'.

Finally on the Place D'Austerlitz, at the western end of the Boulevard General Leclerc, itself an extension of the Cours Grandval, is the one statute of Napoleon that one can take seriously, which is in fact worthy of so great a figure. It is a modern work by Seurre, unveiled on 15 August 1938, the 169th anniversary of his birth; a replica of that which stood on the Colonne Vendome till 1863, and is now to be found in *Les Invalides.* There are no pseudo-classical robes. The Emperor is in his famous *redingote,* the familiar *bicorne* on his head, hand in waistcoat. He stands on a granite eminence staring out to sea, at that element even he could never conquer, and it is there that one can leave him to his meditation, to turn from the past to the present.

The living heart of Ajaccio is the Cours Grandval, prolonged to the west by the Boulevard General Leclerc, to the east by the Avenue de Paris and the Avenue Premier Consul.

Even the disgruntled Lear arriving in rain and blustery winds had to admit 'This Cours Grandval is really fine: a wide carriage road with a footpath on each side, and in its position, high above the sea, most beautiful.' But he goes on to complain of the general drabness of the inhabitants' appearance 'in no wise picturesque or remarkable'. Even between the wars, visitors to the island were struck by the universal black, the perpetual mourning shrouding the women of all ages. This is where Corsica has changed so much in recent years. Young girls are no longer prepared to envelop themselves in mourning for months, even years, in memory of some distant, probably unloved, relation, so that today the crowds in the Cours Grandval are as gaily clad as those of the Promenade des Anglais or the Croisette.

Like all main streets of Mediterranean towns, the Cours abounds with cafés, and to sit on one of the terraces of a spring or summer evening, is to watch living Ajaccio, the Corsica of tomorrow, pass before one's eyes, as the young parade up and down the wide pavements in little groups often arm-in-arm, possible preliminary to some clandestine rendez-vous. This again is a typical Mediterranean institution, though not so much of a rite as in Greece.

The best choice for a first excursion inland is to the Chateau de la Punta, an impressive construction which took eight years to complete (1886-1894), and was planned by the Pozzo di Borgo family, one imagines, to demonstrate the fact that the Bonapartes and the Paolis were not the only great Corsican families of recent times. Just thirteen kilometres from Ajaccio, the chateau – in the true sense of the word rather than a *chateau fort* – occupies a dominating position some 2000 feet above sea level.

The first great member of the family, Charles André, a protégée of Paoli, remained an uncompromising enemy of the Bonapartes all his life, yet was never anti-French, dying in Paris at the age of seventy-eight in 1842, after having served as Russian Ambassador at the Court of both Louis XVIII and Louis Philippe. He was indeed a remarkable man, often described as a 'loyal' opponent for, as Jacques Gregori says speaking of the rivalry between the two Ajaccian families, unlike many of Napoleon's friends and so many who owed all to him – such as Bernadotte, Murat, Talleyrand, and Ney – *'Pozzo ne le* (Napoleon) *trahit jamais pour la bonne raison qu'il le combattit toujours'*.

It was his descendant, Duke Pozzo di Borgo, who had the genial idea of saving something from the ruins of the Tuileries, burnt in 1871 by the *Commune* vandals, the shell later pulled down, for political reasons, on orders of the Third Republic. Columns, stones, marbles, all that could be salvaged, were shipped to Corsica, and with the grilles from the Chateau de Saint Cloud, the imposing Chateau de la Punta was erected. Splendid as is the exterior with its superimposed Ionic and Corinthian columns, the real interest is the inside, its vast rooms, and priceless collection of Louis XV and Empire furniture. There is so much to see that it is worth submitting to the discipline of a guided tour. Hatred of the Bonapartes has not prevented a portrait of Napoleon by David being the show piece of the Grand Salon, eclipsing that of Paoli by Gérard. A more inspired work by the same artist is the portrait of Valentine de Crillon, Duchess Pozzo di Borgo, displayed in the Salon Louis XV. In the dining room, the beams of the ceiling bear the arms of the families allied in marriage to the Pozzo di Borgos, while on the library mantelpiece can be seen two beautiful Saint Petersburg vases, gift to Charles André of the Czar Alexander I.

Cars are not allowed on the road which leads from the Chateau to the headland known as Pointe Pozzo di Borgo, but the distance, there and back, can be covered on foot in little over an hour. About 500 feet higher than the chateau, the view is superb, from that height the sea taking on a green tinge peculiar to Corsican waters and particularly those of the west coast. Below one can see a lower headland, another favourite excursion from Ajaccio, the Pointe de la Parata, with its stubby Genoese watch tower built in 1608, and beyond, a sort of broken extension, the Iles Sanguinaires, which can, as their name suggests, on some evenings as the sun sets, become blood red. The lighthouse on the largest of these islands, the Grande Sanguinaire, was the setting for the *Lettres de mon Moulin*, which Daudet entitled, *L'Agonie de la 'Semillante'*, and *Les Douaniers*. Turning one's back on the sea, the view is perhaps even more grandiose, for, on a clear day, it is a vista of the great peaks, the three giants which watch over Ajaccio, Monte Renoso, Monte d'Oro, and Monte Rotondo. Though not quite as high as Monte Cinto, further north, all three are nearer to 9000 than 8000 feet, and the blood red of a setting sun's rays on those snow covered summits is startling.

Because of the overall restricted area, it would be possible to base oneself on Ajaccio, and cover the whole of the island in a series of one, or at the most two, day excursions but since one of the many of the island's admirable facets is its variety of scene and atmosphere, rapid visits can never do more than give a highly-superficial appreciation. There are, however, many beauty spots in the neighbourhood of Ajaccio; and one does not have to go far from the city centre to make the first contact with the famous *maquis*.

The part the *maquis* plays in the Corsican story is truly extraordinary. It is always there in the physical background, a moral force in the formation of character. It is the embodiment of the spirit of national resistance throughout the centuries with its resurgence as such during the Second World War; the emblem, as haven of the *bandit d'honneur*, of the old national morality, and today a subject over which feelings are sharply, sometimes passionately, divided. For the traditionalist it is still spells romance, but the modern trend is to look on the *maquis* almost as a national pest. Land once forested but ravaged by fires, land once cultivated but neglected for lack of man power or for economic reasons, is invariably 'claimed by the *maquis*', thus becoming the symbol of unproductivity, while today all connections between the words 'bandit' and 'honour' have been severed; crimes of violence in Corsica, as elsewhere in the world, are now simply sordid. Gone indeed are the days when a man like Wyndham Lewis, almost lamenting the death of the outlaw Romanetti (1926), would write 'He had the instinctive courtesy of the Latin mixed with that dash of the theatre, that streak of cabotinage, from which no commanding and romantic public figure is entirely free.'

The younger generation, increasingly modelling itself on the 'continental', tends to reject the bandit tradition, much as the younger Moroccans tend to reject the traditional *jellaba* in favour of a dark suit or blue jeans.

Nevertheless for the visitor, the *maquis,* apart from its 'scent', does possess a certain fascination. Stripped of all romantic phraseology, one could say simply that it was scrubland, yet covered by such varied vegetation that a list of its many species would fill a small catalogue. This scrub varies in height from a few inches to several feet, interspersed by thickets of ilex and cork oak, so that the *maquis* can and did provide that cover the fugitive from justice was seeking, its very denseness making pursuit all the more difficult. Myrtle, arbutus, heather, lentisk, broom – particularly the species known as *genet,* a glorious golden blaze from late April till the end of June – wild lavender, juniper, rosemary, and wild olive, are but a few of the plants of the *maquis* which in its ensemble and seen from a distance, gives the impression of a deep purple fungus invading the countryside.

In all fairness it should be added that the *maquis* is not entirely unproductive. Briar (*bruyère*) roots are used to make briar pipes, many of its blooms attract honey bees, while the myrtle and arbutus serve to produce the incredibly strong *eau-de-vie,* the favourite evening drink in the mountain villages.

To the north of Ajaccio, the wide Sagone Gulf is a good out-of-season area for the person who wants a quiet, relaxed bathing holiday, with its three small resorts of Tiuccia, Sagone, and Cargese. The road, often agreeably traffic free, crosses the spur of mountains separating the Taravo and

Prunelli valleys by the Col de San Bastiano where there is a pinky coloured stèle commemorating the fact that it was as long ago as November 1886 that the first successful crossing of part of the Mediterranean was made by air. Two very brave men, Alphonse Fondère and Louis Capazza, on board a balloon they had christened the *Gabizos* left Marseille and after what was a most perilous flight, were extremely lucky to land intact at night in the neighbourhood.

It is in the Gulf of Sagone, that one first makes the acquaintance of the island's violent past. Tiuccia spread along a fine sandy *plage,* is overlooked by the crumbling ruins of Capraja Castle, the home of the great Cinarca family, once the most powerful in the land. Few families anywhere in the world have had a more turbulent, bloody, history. The setting for the ruins could scarcely be more peaceful, but there is a lurking sense of oppression as though the ghosts of the Cinarchesi are still tied to the scenes of so much bloodshed, treachery and tragedy. One thinks above all of Sinucello Della Rocca, betrayed to the Genoese by his own son and sent to rot in a Genoese prison. All these Cinarchesi seemed to have been moulded to a set character pattern; fearless in battle, inspired by ideals, yet equally blinded by hatreds, self-seeking and yet willing to sacrifice themselves for mere prejudice, and all persecuted by what Napoleon III was to describe as 'the torments of the flesh' which so often, after having sowed a liberal crop of bastards, would, as in the case of Vincentello d'Istria, bring them to ruin and violent death.

Sagone is another deceptive place. Like Tiuccia, on the surface a *port de plaisance,* of almost pert modern aspect, it has a sad, mysterious, history. In late Roman times it was a bishopric. From study of its ruins, the cathedral later built by the Pisans was a magnificent edifice. The Bishop, with twelve parishes in his diocese, was suffragan to the Archbishop of Pisa. Obviously for a time it was one of the richest, most populous, of the island cities. But at some time, and there is no trace of how or by whom – though the theory usually adopted is that it was the Saracens – the city was destroyed. All that is known is that already by the mid-sixteenth century it was nothing but a shell, and that in 1572, Pope Gregory XIII gave permission for the Bishop to install himself at Notre Dame de Vico. The arrangement was only temporary and in 1625, Urban VIII officially transferred the bishopric to Calvi.

It is a popular story that one of the Bishops of Sagone was responsible for a flourishing vineyard on the banks of the Calenzana river being converted overnight into a desolate marsh. The Bishop, unnamed, despite his position was violently attracted by a pretty young village girl who, in turn was well aware of her own charms, and was even able to persuade the Bishop to place his episcopal ring on her finger, but, as he tried to do so, the ring slipped from his grasp, fell to the ground and could not be found. The worried Bishop returned the following morning to the vineyard which had been the scene of their rendez-vous, to find to his horror that the vines had vanished and in their place was an insalubrious swamp.

The first thing one notices when climbing up to the two orchard covered hills on which the town of Cargese sprawls, is the fact that there are two churches, one on each of the humps separated by a narrow valley or hollow. The little town is indeed a friendly meeting place of the two oldest branches of the Christian faith, Orthodox and Roman Catholic, for centuries uncompromisingly opposed the one to the other. To begin with the original Orthodox settlers, Greeks fleeing from the Turks, arrived in Genoa and were granted land in Corsica, not so much for humanitarian reasons, but so as to create a pro-Genoese, anti-native element on the island. The first of these new colonists moved into the territory allotted to them in the neighbourhood of Paomia, a few miles inland and now in ruins, in 1677. They did not stay long. The murder of one of their number by young men from Vico was the prelude to a series of aggressions which ended in the burning of the village and the flight of the survivors to Ajaccio. It was the French, confirmed Philhellenes, at the time of General de Marbeuf's governorship, who had the village of Cargese and its Greek church built in 1774 to create a home for 110 Greek families. They had come to stay. Though to begin with they were ferociously hellenic – only Greek was spoken, only Greek costume worn, only the Orthodox rites celebrated – there were no serious clashes with the neighbouring Corsicans, and gradually the process of integration was set in motion, so much so that today I doubt whether any Cargesian would understand Greek any better than he does Chinese.

In the nineteenth century, some eighty families, it was estimated, attracted by the thought of virgin lands to be claimed, emigrated to Algeria, creating their own village, Sidi Merouan. With the end of the bitter war in Algeria, and following on de Gaulle's decision that *Algérie Francaise* was no longer viable in an increasingly anti-colonial world, 150 descendants of the original families retraced their footsteps to swell the ranks of those generally known as *les Pieds Noirs*.

Though their rites differ, the two churches have one thing in common. Both shelter attractive images of Saint John the Baptist. That in the Orthodox church is a typical Byzantine icon, the Saint's features sharp with an El Greco clarity of line, the eyes staring, over-large yet strangely compelling, the work of a Mount Athos monk, dating it is believed from the sixteenth century. That in the Latin church is undoubtedly older, and Saint John forms part of a group with the Virgin Mary, Saint Elizabeth and the child Christ, the *trompe l'oeil* creation of an anonymous artist.

On the headland is another of the innumerable Genoese watch towers which are such a feature of the landscape. These towers were not part of the defensive system to protect Genoese occupying forces against the depradations of the native Corsicans, but against Saracens and pirates, the scourge of the western Mediterranean.

All have a certain uniformity of construction; round, varying from twelve to seventeen metres in height, they have only one means of access, a small door, normally on the land side, well above ground level. A ladder would be let down, and once the small guard – usually an NCO and three men – had been changed, the ladder was pulled up and the door firmly closed. Originated at the time the island was under the rule of the Bank of Saint George, they served purely as an alarm system – 'As soon as the Barbary sails were spotted by the watchers, the fires which they lit on the roof warned the hill villages of the hinterland, and also, one by one, all the other towers on the coast. It was reckoned that within an hour, the whole island, or at least the coastal regions, knew that the pirates had been sighted.'

In some places the Genoese towers are complemented by larger, square constructions raised by the local inhabitants to shelter the populations of otherwise indefensible villages, and to act as isolated centres of resistance. Neglected once the pirate menace had finally been removed, and of no particular architectural merit, they have been slowly crumbling into ruins. Now the Administration in Corsica is offering these towers to rent for a minimum sum provided the prospective tenant, though given *carte blanche* as to the modernization of the interior, agrees to undertake the restoration of the facade in its original form. The idea has its attractions since the towers are sited to command superb views of sea and coast.

Only twenty kilometres of roads winding through orchards separate Cargese from Piana, gate to one of the most lovely of Corsica's many beautiful areas. A village of just under 800 inhabitants, it dominates the Gulf of Porto, perhaps the most dramatic of the west coast gulfs, where the mountains and sheer rocks plunge dizzily into the sea in a blaze of colour. Red is the major hue; a vivid firm red, far more brilliant than the shades Cézanne was always discovering and re-discovering in the slopes and folds of the Montagne de la Sainte Victoire. It is the red of one of the most remarkable natural phenomena not only of Corsica, but of Europe; Les Calanches (les Calanques). These pointed scarlet granite needles of rock are sometimes as much as a thousand feet sheer, the work of erosion. There are other places where similar giant natural spearpoints can be seen, notably the Plain of Thessaly's *meteora*, but nowhere else do they attain the same exuberant mass, and nowhere else has nature sculpted such utterly fantastic shapes.

This is not something just to be seen cursorily, particularly as Les Calanques are best appreciated at sunset when the staggering colours are even more flamboyantly exaggerated. Stay two or three days using Piana as a base rather than Porto, for although the latter offers a far greater choice of hotels and restaurants, it tends to be over full of tourists and prices rise steadily.

This is the region for someone not so much interested in the works of man, but in the hand of Nature, for Piana and Porto stand at the entrance of the Spelunca Gorges, through which a road leads to the still unspoilt village of Evisa, itself on the threshold of one of the island's loveliest forests, the Aitone. It would be difficult to find a more attractive site than that of Evisa which guide books speak of as *La Perle de la Corse!* Sloping steeply like the typical fortress village, its houses cluster together tightly on the spur separating the Porto river valley and the narrow ravine of the Aitone torrent. Though the normal population, according to the census, is only 631, it is such a perfect retreat for anyone seeking quiet that it now boasts four hotels, where both accommodation and food are what is known – most expressive qualification – as 'honest'. There is no night life, but this matters little when the reason for spending a few days in the village is to use it as a base for excursions on foot.

Only about a kilometre down the Porto road is a magnificent view point, at the spot known as the Tournant de Saint-Cyprien. From there you have the dramatic blend of sea, mountain, valley, rock and forest. Though not in the main chestnut producing area, La Castigniccia, Evisa is ringed by chestnut trees, and their lush summer green contrasts vividly with stark red rock, dark hills, the distant shimmering Mediterranean, and 'wild and gloomy precipices'. If one feature steals the picture, it is perhaps the Spelunca pinnacle, spire of the gorges which are well worth an individual visit, seen at their best if one is prepared to spend most of a day on foot negotiating steep, often slippery, mule tracks.

Dizziness may be a hazard on a tour of Provence's famous Gorges du Verdon, for though there are negotiable tracks following the Verdon river's turgid course, most people take the motor road which circles the cliff heights. In the Spelunca gorges, on the other hand, sightseers strain their neck muscles looking up the sheer rock face, and feeling uncomfortably dwarfed. This gorge gives the impression that in its design, Nature must have consulted the unborn spirit of Bernard Buffet, for the base seems so narrow, the towering pinnacles so elongated, as to appear the work of some monstrous compressor.

It is only another eleven kilometres from Evisa, climbing steadily, to the Col di Vergio at 4800 feet, the highest point attainted by a motor road in Corsica, passing through the lovely pine forest of Aitone. These pines, known as *laricio,* are not the somewhat stunted growths one generally associates with the Mediterranean coasts. Many of the trees are giants, reminiscent of Austria's Carinthian forests, and as a variation, there are independent copses of beech trees which in spring lighten the overall sombre mood of the dark pines by the sparkling, almost translucent green of their young sprouting leaves catching the sun. A few steps from the road lead to a world of mysterious shadows and rustling. Round the barrier of any trunk one would not be surprised to run into some Corsican elf or hermit; or a truculent wild boar.

On the *col* itself, the view is somewhat obscured, but a short climb to a rocky ledge to the left (north west) gives a tremendous prospect over the eastern slopes, the great rival forest, that of Valdo Niello, and the Golo river valley, down to the Tyrrhenian sea, while to the north is the great 9000-foot peak of Monte Cinto. It is no wonder that in such a region, the visionary outlaw, Teodoro Poli, should have conceived the idea of proclaiming himself the 'King of the Mountains', confident that his realm would never be violated.

8　Calvi: *Semper Fidelis*

On 22 May 1794, Bastia surrendered after being bombarded by Admiral Hood's fleet and invested by a mixed force of Corsicans and of British regular army units; 200 men of the Royals, the 50th, 51st, and 69th regiments of foot, commanded by Brigadier-General D'Aubant. Once Bastia had fallen, Calvi was the next objective. The Corsicans marched overland, but the British, numbering some 2500, this time commanded by Lieutenant-Colonel Moore – later Sir John Moore, whose burial at Corunna was immortalized in verse – were taken by ship to the west coast, where, reinforced by special flank companies of the Royal Irish and naval landing parties, overall command was assumed by General Charles Stuart. The naval detachment, under Captain Nelson, was to assist in the assault on the village of Mozzello, perched on a rocky plateau overlooking Calvi, from which position his guns could fire directly down on the French defences.

The bombardment opened on 4 July. Nelson was observing the effects of the naval salvos, when a nearby explosion threw up a shower of rock splinters, one of which blinded him in the right eye, an infirmity he was later able to turn to his advantage at Copenhagen. The French, commanded by General Casabianca, a pro-Bonaparte Corsican, put up a strong resistance and it was not till 10 August, by which time, according to Moore, 'the whole town was a heap of ruins' that Casabianca agreed to surrender provided the garrison were accorded 'the honour of war'.

The old city is a fine example of the inherent Genoese

genius for military architecture. Built on the summit of an arm of land pushing out into the sea, the rock formations incorporated in the walls, it gives the impression of being almost impregnable in the days before modern artillery and aerial bombardment. This blend of natural and man-made fortification does not however, minimize the gallantry of both garrison and civilian population displayed during the ordeals of siege.

Though there was an habitation on the same site, the scene of Saint Restitute's martyrdom, at the dawn of the Christian era, in its present form Calvi was founded by the pro-Genoese Corsican Giovanninello de Loreto in 1268. With Bonifacio, it was to become a major centre of Genoese influence. Only in these two cities did they feel confident of holding out against the successive tides of revolt against their presence, periodically convulsing the island.

Today old Calvi has been pushed into the background due to the fact that it is the most popular of the island's summer resorts; the Cannes, as it were, of Corsica. Though the local population numbers a bare 3000, there are three hotels classed as 'palaces', and a number of expensive restaurants which can compare with those of the Promenade des Anglais and the Croisette. Since the port is well sheltered, it is also a favourite anchorage for tax dodgers' yachts while the great curve of the *plage* is always packed by those whose ideal is an occasional dip in shallow water in the intervals of cooking on the sand. In the season it is a riot of bodies, tents, umbrellas, a faithful reproduction of any Mediterranean resort since the post-war discovery of the sun. Yet old Calvi though seemingly forgotten, retains a magic charm, an underlying quality of indestructability.

Though one can take a car as far as the cathedral church of Saint John the Baptist the citadel should be visited on foot, for then the absence of noise in the narrow streets and alleys, shaded by the high walls of austere houses, is a spiritual bridge spanning the ravine separating the past and the present.

The old palace, once the seat of the Genoese Governor,

overlooking the Place d'Armes, has been taken over as a barracks for the Foreign Legion who moved in in 1962 after General de Gaulle had decided that *Algérie Française* was no longer a viable proposition. With a heavy heart the Legion said good-bye to its famous depot at Sidi-bel-Abbes, closing a volume covering 131 years of service in Africa, to start anew at Aubagne, half way between Marseille and Aix-en-Provence.

Most of the *légionnaires* in Corsica belong to the 2nd Parachute Regiment (*Le Deuxième* REP). Because of the hair-raising reputation of *légionnaires* – and especially legion parachutists – for brutal toughness acquired, thanks to a bizarre mixture of the works of starry-eyed romantic novelists and left-wing propaganda, their arrival was dreaded and resented. It was not long, however, before the mistrustful local population came to realise their fears had been groundless, that the 'paras' and other *légionnaires* were not a band of drunken rapists systematically sewing terror and destruction on their path every pay night. Highly disciplined, taking an intense, almost fanatical pride in their unit, they soon made themselves universally liked and respected. Their presence undoubtedly adds a touch of colour and romance to city life, while the annual festival of Camerone*, makes 30 April the most eagerly awaited of the year's events.

The cathedral church of Saint John the Baptist, completed in the thirteenth century and largely restored in 1578 after having taken a fearful battering in the 1553 siege, is on the far side of the Place d'Armes. There is a reminder of the great siege on the altar to the right of the choir, the statue, the 'Christ of the Miracles', for it was at a moment when it seemed that a savage Turkish attack was likely to gain a footing on the ramparts, that the Christ was held up over the head of one of the defenders. At the sight of the relic the Turks halted, broke off the assault falling back in disorder, never to reform. The city was saved.

---

* On 30 April 1863, at Camerone in Mexico, 64 *légionnaires* held out for 12 hours against 3000 Mexicans thus protecting a bullion convoy. Only two survived. The day is celebrated as the *Fète de La Légion*.

Above the marble-inlaid high altar is a triptych, work of one of Genoa's best-known artists, Barbagelata. Dated 1498, it is a copy of an identical work by his master Giovanni Mazone, housed in Genoa's church of Santa Maria di Castello. The centre panel is missing, possibly due to war damage, and has been replaced by a figure of the Baptist, but the side panels, representing the Annunciation and the figures of six saints, are vivid examples of 'primitive' art.

The series of boxes, protected by grilles, vaguely reminiscent of Kashmiri balconies, situated below the central cupola, are not, as might be imagined, novel confessionals. In the days when women were very much the chattels of their masters, their purpose was to protect the wives of prominent citizens from the lustful gazes, real or imaginary, of the hoi pollio, during the celebration of Mass.

Below the cupola is the tomb of the Baglioni family, extolled as defenders of liberty. Bayon Baglioni is the first remembered of the family. In 1400, the war which opposed Arrigo della Rocca, backed from time to time by Aragonese contingents, to Genoa, had been raging for fifteen years. Calvi was one of the few places which had managed to hold out against Arrigo and his 'patriots'. Nevertheless there were amongst its citizens a number who wished to see the end of Genoese rule. As he was leaving the church one Sunday morning, Bayon overheard two men discussing the possibility of opening the city gates at night and letting in the Aragonese detachment in the neighbourhood. Not a man to argue or ask questions, Bayon promptly drew his sword, and to cries of *'Liberta! Liberta!'* cut down the two plotters, a couple of murders which earned the family the right to call itself, from then on, Baglioni-Liberta. Baglioni, as can be deduced from his action was an enthusiastic supporter of Genoa, mortal enemy of Arrigo and this 'patriot' movement and thus a strange candidate for a national hero. Moving to Marseille in the middle of the sixteenth century, a group of three Baglioni-Liberta brothers repeated Bayon's gesture, killing 'the Quisling who was about to surrender the town to a besieging Spanish fleet'.

Two men of world-wide fame are claimed, locally, to be

originaires of Calvi; the explorer Cristoph Colomb, and the most celebrated of lovers, Don Juan.

Set in the wall of the narrow Rue Colombo is a modest, almost apologetic plaque:

Ville de Calvi
Ici est né en 1441
CHRISTOPHE COLOMB*
Immortalisé par la découverte du Nouveau Monde
Alors que Calvi était sous la domination Gênoise;
Mort à Valladolid, le 20 Mai, 1500

This claim is generally denied by historians the world over, though Corsicans put in a counter claim that the Genoese destroyed the original records so that their city could boast of being the explorer's birthplace. My only comment is that should by any chance the plaque be telling the truth,then the memorial to the birth of the man who first sighted the 'New World' on 12 October 1492 compares very unfavourably with that to his death, the magnificent bronze group in Sevilla's La Giralda cathedral of his coffin being borne on the shoulders of the four Kings of Spain; a tardy recognition of his achievements after the ungrateful King Ferdinand had allowed him to die in near indigence.

Strangely enough the real Don Juan followed, rather than preceded, the fictional hero – or anti-hero – Don Juan, central character of Molino's play, *El Burlador de Sevilla,* an unprecedented success at the time of its production in 1621. It was still being performed many years after the birth in Sevilla in 1627, of Miguel de Leca y Colonna y Manara, son of Tomaso and Jeronima (née Anfriani) Manara, both of Calvi, who had emigrated to Spain the previous year. At a very early age, Miguel was allowed to see the play, and was so impressed that he determined to outdo the Don. He was still in his teens when amongst his friends he was invariably referred to as Don

---

* This of course is the French spelling. Otherwise should we stick to the more popular English – Christopher Columbus?

Juan, far surpassing the fictional hero's amatory prowess. His many scabrous exploits in his career of the seduction of 'the most inaccessible married women and young girls'; included the killing – as in the play – of one outraged father, the murder of a brother to whom he had deliberately disclosed the rendez-vous with his sister, and the attempted rape of a half-sister'. This super-rake's progress, however, ended as abruptly as it had begun when the real-life Don Juan was only twenty-one. His conversion, beginning with a number of eerie, supernatural experiences when he had embarked on the seduction of a nun who would, one understands, have been a very willing sinner, was completed by marriage to the fourteen-year-old Jeronima Carillo de Mendoza, 'as pure as she was beautiful'.

Miguel (Don Juan) settled down to be a model husband and citizen till, in 1661, Jeronima died very suddenly. This tragedy did not, as might have been expected, plunge him back into his life as a debauchée. Instead, after nearly dying of grief, he joined the fraternity of the *Santa Caridad*. From then on, after the pattern of the late-nineteenth century rake-turned-saint, Charles de Foucauld, he devoted himself to the poor, indifferent to his own needs, impervious to his own safety, till his death in 1679.

It has been remarked, rather sadly, that it is the Miguel-Don Juan, rather than Saint Miguel, who has left his mark on the Calvi young, for Calvi youths are reputed to be the most 'dashing', to use an old-fashioned expression, and pleasure loving on the island.

To return to the lower town is, in fact, to make a journey of centuries in a few steps. It is almost impossible to believe that Calvi has only some 3000 inhabitants, with its luxury hotels, excellent restaurants and cafés lining the palm and *platane*-shaded Place Christophe Colomb, and the Boulevard Wilson, as proud of its shops as the Cannebière, the joy of all *Marseillais*. This modern Calvi seems to be ambitiously on the fringe of rejecting history to take her place on the list of the jet-age pleasure resorts; a Corsican Acapulco, contrasting strongly with the description by Major Dugmore in the twenties: 'When I visited Calvi there was no real hotel such as the one recently built, the one I had the misfortune to try had better not be described.'

Nearby Ile Rousse (Isola Rossa), founded by Pasquale Paoli in 1758 as 'the gibbet from which to hang Calvi', would like to rival this claim to ultra-sophistication, but somehow it still keeps the air of a *parvenu,* striving, but not altogether successfully to gain an aura of tradition. It may be the fact that, unique among Corsican towns, Ile Rousse does not boast a citadel, that makes it something of an urban black sheep. No house bears a plaque to remind the visitor that it was the birthplace of some island hero or site of some heroic deed. The only family mentioned in connection with the town's history is is that of the Arenas, and theirs is a tale of misfortune. Barthélemy Arena, one of the islands's representatives in Revolutionary Paris was bitterly opposed to Napoleon's *coup d'état* of the eighteenth *Brumaire.* He was lucky to escape from France, reach Livorno, and there die in obscurity. His brother Joseph, also a deputy, was less fortunate. Accused of plotting the murder of Napoleon when First Consul, he perished on the scaffold with Cadoudal. Always apparently on the wrong side of the fence, the family home was burnt down by Paolists but rebuilt after the restoration in 1819.

Known for a time as Paolina, then Vaux, after the Marquis de Vaux, victor of Ponte Nuovo, Ile Rousse owes its actual name to a cluster of red granite islets. The largest and nearest to the mainland is La Pietra or Isola Rossa, being reached by a bridge which is a favourite evening stroll.

Tradition may be lacking, but there is certainly an air of material prosperity, and the little port plays an important role in Corsican economy as the centre to which the olive oil and citrus fruits of the Balagne hinterland is directed for export. Traditionally one of the richest corners of the island, the Balagne has been hard-hit recently by emigration and a series of devastating fires, together with an alarming decline in the demand for olive oil. This recession, however, is expected to be ended by the vast increase in tourism, and the inauguration of a hydro-electric scheme.

From the tourist's point of view, the Balagne is known to possess many of the best examples of Pisan ecclesiastical architecture. Every smallest village is endowed with a lovely little church. In fact the region is sometimes referred to as *Sainte Balagne*. Largest of the villages, Calenzana is only thirteen kilometres inland from Calvi, yet utterly divorced from the coastal atmosphere. Its tightly-packed houses are dwarfed by a towering campanile, in turn overshadowed by the craggy hill at whose foot it stands, and like so many Corsican villages, is almost encircled by two fast-running streams, the Secco and the Bartasca.

Reaching the village, one sees that the campanile stands on its own, in the centre of a cemetery known as the *Campu Santu dei Tedeschi* (the Holy Field, or cemetery, of the Germans). The Germans buried here are not casualties of the Second World War, but of the 1731 campaign when the Genoese enlisted the help of the Emperor Charles VI, during the course of which the village was the scene of a sharp, bloody, encounter on 14 January 1732. There are two opposing versions of the engagement which resulted in the death of the 500 Germans buried in the churchyard to which they have given their name.

According to Colonel von Loewendhal, present on the day – 'As soon as the (German) detachments entered the village, they were attacked from all sides, the enemy firing on them from windows, doors, and the roofs of all the houses, which are flat, and hurling stones down on them, in this latter activity the women being particularly conspicuous. Soon the enemy numbered at least 7000. [Probably a gross exaggeration. The number might even have been as low as 700.] The houses would not catch fire and soon, suffering heavy casualties, we were obliged to fall back towards Calvi harried for at least two miles by the rebels.'

The Corsican version is more picturesque. It stresses that the villagers gave no sign of life, thus luring the Germans into the narrow streets and alleys. When they reached the village centre, the inhabitants who had been hiding on the roofs, bombarded them with bee hives. Maddened by thousands of stings, the Germans threw away their arms and rushed for the fountains, where they were attacked and butchered by villagers armed with axes and knives.

Which is the true version? As Jacques Gregori says 'Only the dead reposing in the *Campu Santu dei Tedeschi* can give the answer'.

The church itself is seventeenth century, erected on the site of the original Romanesque construction. The interior, plainer than most churches of the period, has no striking paintings to catch the eye. Only a kilometre further on, however, to the left of the road in a typical setting of olive groves, is the Church of Saint Restitute, a Corsican martyr beheaded in 303 on the order of Diocletian. The church dates back to the eleventh century, but the original has been added to, and the whole exterior covered with a glaring white wash.

Restitute's white marble sarcophagus was discovered by excavators working on the site, knowing it to be that of a Roman necropolis, who were able to identify it as of the fourth century. Possibly because of the melancholy increase of acts of vandalism, principally on the part of tourists, the door is kept locked, and a visit has to be arranged with the Curé of Calenzana. What is interesting is that, probably in the fifteenth century, the sarcophagus was enclosed in a false cenotaph covered with frescoes depicting the martyrdom painted in the 'primitive' style, and which one expert thinks may have been copies of an original work on the same subject. The Romans are dressed in medieval costume, while the execution scene shows that Saint Restitute's fate was shared by five companions. It was only in 1951 that the true sarcophagus was discovered.

Continuing north on the N844, the road is a succession of view-points and Pisan churches, harmonious blend of the natural and the man-made. Montemaggiore, birthplace of the real Don Juan's mother, with its delicate baroque church and campanile, is a gem amongst *villages perchés*. From the *place*, a superb panorama embraces the Secco valley with its ocean of olive trees reminiscent of Delphi, Calvi's distant ramparts, and beyond the truly green Mediterranean.

There is a climb to the *col* (or *bocca*) San Cesareo, and

continuing along the N844, turn right to Sant'Antonio – or Sant-Antonino, as it is marked on some maps – a distance of some two kilometres. This time from the centre of the pyramidal village on the ridge dominating the Regino valley, look inland, to the island's centre. Here hills and mountains crowd in, some bare and craggy, some heather, *maquis* covered, others dark with chestnut groves and pine forests. This is real Corsica. Even in this day and age one hears Corse spoken. A number of the old men wear traditional Balkan-like clothes; inevitably the majority of the women are in black, many with the gnarled skin and rugged features peculiar to mountain people, that may denote any age from forty to 100.

After this diversion, visit the church of Aregno, the Holy Trinity, for it is quite one of the finest of the Pisan-Romanesque style.

The most striking feature of the exterior is its rigid simplicity and the fact that the walls resemble, the profane might suggest, a giant pattern of chess boards, with their alternating black and white granite slabs, giving what the erudite term an 'irridescent polychrome effect'. There is no stained glass, no sculpture, no riot of frieze, such as makes the glory of many of the Provençal churches. The great main door might be described as strictly utilitarian, though its arch has two small figures, a male and a female, one on either side of the base, and above, four harmonious blind arcades, the capitals of whose pilasters are decorated with bas-reliefs, representing some vague form of quadruped.

The chief interest of the plain, dark, timbered, interior, is the north wall which has two mid-fifteenth century frescos, work of an anonymous Corsican; Saint Michael Slaying a Dragon; and The Four Doctors of the Church.

This little tour is best ended by a visit to the village of Corbara and its immediate surroundings, a village overlooking Ile Rousse, sprawled over the slopes of Mont de Guido, and dominated by the ruins of a castle, family home of the Savellis, who claim descent from a Roman Prince who emigrated from the mainland in the ninth century. Soon establishing themselves as one of the great families of the

Balagne, the Savellis assumed the title of Count of Balagne after being the architects of numerous victories over the Saracens. The castle whose ruins we see was completed by Count Mannone Savelli, one of the greatest scourges of the predatory North African Moslems. Intensely Corsican despite their Italian origin, the Savellis were always sworn enemies of the Genoese, and later when the Corsicans themselves were torn by rival factions, allied themselves with Paoli rather than Bonaparte. Their basic anti-republicanism also earned them the enmity of Berthélemy Arena who ordered their more modern residence, the Castel du Guido, to be razed in 1798. Later restored, the manor now houses a collection of paintings and Florentine furniture of considerable value. Steps hewn into the solid rock lead up to what was once the entrance of the ruined castle of Corbara just beyond Corbara village, above which can still be seen the carved inscription of the disciples at Emmaus – *Tu es peregrinus solus in Hierusalem.*

Before the village is the *Couvent de Corbara,* a Franciscan monastery founded in 1456. The peaceful Franciscans were driven out in 1792, victims of revolutionary cant, but in 1857 the semi-ruin was taken over by the Dominicans who turned it into a philosophical and theological college. Many of the Order's most famous men taught there, including Father Didon, a friend of Guy de Maupassant, a man whose ideas were considered so 'liberal' for the time that he was transferred from Paris to the wilds of Corsica where, it was felt, he would have less opportunity for propagating his doctrines. Never a man to waste time in regrets, Father Didon used his years in 'exile' to write a thoughtful profound and deeply-moving *Vie de Jésus.*

From the monastery, it takes less than an hour to climb to the top of Monte Sant'Angelo, with yet another breath-taking view-point. Most of the Balagne is spread out below, and on a clear winter day, locals insist, the snows of the *Alpes Maritimes* are clearly visible. Though I have never had the luck to strike a clear enough day, I well remember one brilliant January afternoon, seeing the peak of Monte Cinto from the terrace of a café of Eze Village on the *moyenne corniche,* between

Villefranche and Monte Carlo. On that day, locals told me that it was a phenomenon likely to occur only once every fifty years.

Corbara village has a fascinating Barbary Coast aspect. It might be anywhere in the Riff country beyond Tetuan with its solid, square, flat-roofed houses and hedges of prickly pear. At any moment I expected to see a group of Riffians appear from the rocks, in short brown *jellabas* and sombrero-like straw hats embellished with coloured wool bobbles. The connection is probably more than fantasy, for the Balagne was a favourite Saracen objective.

Another unspoilt area of the Calvi-Ile Rousse hinterland is that of Asco, giving its name to a village, a river, a forest, and a spectacular gorge, lying to the south east of Calenzana. Ascans claim to be of pure Ligurian stock, true Corsicans whose blood has never been polluted by that of the island's many invaders. This immunity they owed to their territory's difficult access, but where Saracens, Pisans, and Genoese may have failed, the modern internationalists have succeeded. At a height of 6000 feet, Haut Asco is now a small winter sports centre, and a point of departure for organized ascents of Monte Cinto, the island's highest peak. I have not made the climb myself, but am told that the view from the summit more than recompenses the backbreaking efforts involved.

Today, the Asco region is best approached from the east, one excellent road branching from the N197 just north of Ponte Leccia. Much of it is now part of the National Park, 3000 hectares (7500 acres) being a reserve for the rare moufflon, described in Bewick's *History of Quadrupeds* as 'Moufflon or Musmon, animal neither sheep nor goat; hair, no wool: horns like those of a ram . . . found in wild and uncultured parts of Greece, Sardinia, Corsica, and in the deserts of Tartary . . . fearful of mankind'. It is thanks to this Park, curtailing the Tartarin instincts of Corsicans and visitors to Corsica alike, that island wild life today seems to have some hope of survival, for the whole Park which covers 150,000 hectares, about one-fifth of the island's total superficies, also shelters lynx, deer, and wild boar. Hunting

22 *BONIFACIO harbour*

parties can be arranged to kill off superfluous boar, but the moufflon enjoys a sacrosanct protection, similar to that of India's sacred cow.

The people of Asco Village, eighteen kilometres from Ponte Leccia, enjoyed a remote individuality till the opening of the road in 1937. Travelling up the shadowy Asco gorge, with its jagged perpendicular rock faces towering 3000 feet above the road, one can well understand why it was that valley communities were so isolated due to the total absence of lateral communications, and why village life, as a result, inevitably turned inwards instead of looking to the outside world.

Asco village is still compared by some with a monastic settlement, 'the ideal spot for a retreat', and is indeed the end of the road, for only a few kilometres farther on, the rough D147 peters out in an area seemingly so remote and savage that one might well be lost in the heart of some unknown continent.

9 Corte

An island on the edge of gigantic cliffs

Of Corsica's three capitals, Corte was the most truly Corsican by reason of its creation as a symbol of the island's will to independence; its refusal to bow to a foreign yoke. Bastia always symbolized, and still does to a certain extent, Genoese rule, while Ajaccio's rise to pre-eminence really started as a family affair, and remains the capital, the Imperial City, as a reminder that an Ajaccian once ruled from Paris not only France, but all continental Europe. Corte, on the other hand, is traditional Corsica, the Corsica of the 'patriots' and the heroes – Vincentello d'Istria, Sampiero, and Pasquale Paoli. In direct contrast to Calvi and Bonifacio, it was a city the Genoese could never hold, let alone subdue. Not only spiritually, but geographically, it is the natural capital. It rises up from the island's heart dominating the main north-south central road, which more or less bisects it, as well as a network of roads, valleys, and passes, polarizing east-west communications, a natural fortress, surging from the valley – 'an island on the edge of gigantic cliffs' – almost encircled by the Tavignano and Retonica rivers.

For a first sight of the still austere city – although counting only 5491 inhabitants, the word 'town' seems ill applied – the southern access via Venaco and Vivario is preferable, because not only is the landscape intensely dramatic, but because both of these towns is, each in its way, a separate pearl in the chain of the island's beauty spots. Vivario, in the Vecchio valley, has been described by Ardouin-Dumazet as truly Alpine in a setting 'more elegant (than the Alps themselves), more majestic, thanks to the brilliant clear sky and the transparent luminosity of its dancing cascades'. Venaco, favourite hot-weather resort for the inhabitants of both Bastia and Ajaccio is a green oasis framed by chestnut trees and wide pastures, ideal grazing for the island's fattest flocks of sheep.

The origin of Corte is allegedly Saracen dating back to the eighth century, but from the Corsican point of view, Corte was born when the existing town was seized by Vincentello d'Istria in 1419, after his great victory over the Genoese at Morosaglia, and the construction of the citadel begun on his orders. Recaptured by the Genoese after Vincentello's death, then handed over to the Bank of Saint George, this dark period of foreign occupation ended in 1553, after a combined Franco-Patriot army had landed under the overall command of the Marshal de Thermes, and the people of Corte had opened the city gates to welcome Sampiero. The city changed hands several times over the next 150 years, but even when occupied by the invader, remained fiercely nationalistic, waiting for the first opportunity to rise in revolt.

On 11 May 1732, after the campaign which had opposed Corsican patriots to combined Genoese and Austro-German forces, representatives of Corsica, Genoa and Austria met at Corte to work out terms of a Treaty. Only two years later armed rebellion flared up all over the island led by Giacinto Paoli, Pasquale's father, sparking off a long, unbelievably bitter war which ended, and then only temporarily, when Corte was chosen by Pasquale Paoli as his capital, after being elected leader of the Corsican people on 13 July 1755, with the title 'General of the Corsican Nation'. It was also in Corte that his 'Constitution' was officially adopted, the Constitution so admired by J. J. Rousseau, that he gave it as his opinion that in all Europe, only the Corsicans were fit to rule themselves.

Corte fell to the French after the fatal battle of Ponte Nuovo which sounded the knell of the dream of independent Corsica. After twenty years spent mostly in London, Paoli returned when Paris decreed an amnesty for 'rebel' Corsicans, then quarrelling with France, called on Britain for help. It was in

Corte that the island was declared a part of the British Empire, and turning to the British representative, Sir Gilbert Elliott, Paoli exclaimed *'Enfin ma chere petite patrie a trouvé un refuge permanent dans le coeur du Roi d'Angleterre'*. ('At last my beloved little country has found a lasting haven in the King of England's heart.')

This short-lived honeymoon was Corte's last moment of national and international glory. With the return of France, and the establishment of Ajaccio, Corte lapsed into the status of minor provincial centre brooding on its heroic past; an attraction for only the more venturesome tourist or the historian.

As a city the interest is not so much visual, once the impressive framework has been assimilated, but in associations with the past. Apart from the citadel, the old town buildings are characterless, of no architectural significance, while the lower town is being victimized by the construction of the standard hideous blocks of offices and flats in disharmony with the surroundings.

Lear, only interested in subjects for his canvases, hated the place, although admitting the beauty of 'the general aspect of the exterior'. He complains, of being impolitely treated 'I had been told the people of Corte had the reputation of being more turbulent than any in the island', and on his departure says spitefully 'Adieu, Corte. . . . until cleanliness is in a greater degree recognized as a virtue, I should not wish to make any of your houses my home.' Major Dugmore, usually so enthusiastic, comments 'if there is architectural talent, it hides its light under a very efficient bushel'.

On the other hand, no place I have visited has more atmosphere. Even without pre-knowledge of history, one can sense the violent past, the fact that the narrow streets, dark unfriendly frontages, bleak *places,* silent stone stairways, have been the scenes of murder, battle, treachery, triumph and despair; and because the city's story is so uniquely military, the presence of white-kepied Legionaries brings an extra touch of authenticity. Their barracks are the old citadel of Vincentello, hanging like an eagle's nest on its crag above the

Tavignano river, and here, as in Calvi, their originally dreaded arrival has been a boon to local tradesmen, and provided husbands for a number of local girls. On the Place du Poilu, is the house where Madame Mère gave birth to the eldest of her five sons, Joseph, later King of Spain, actually the family home of one of Napoleon's most talented leaders, Arrighi de Casanove, later Duke of Padua and Governor of Corsica during the Hundred Days.

The true centre of Corte, however, is the Place Gaffori, named after General Gaffori (1704-1753), known sometimes as *Le Chef suprème des Corses,* with its modern (1901) bronze statue, work of the sculptor Aldebert. The Maison Gaffori, where the general was born, on the north corner of the Place and opposite the church of the Annunciation, still displays a bullet-pitted wall, reminding one of the moment when the indomitable Madame Faustine Gaffori, besieged by the Genoese, threatened to blow up the house and everybody in it, if the word surrender were ever breathed. The house of the Romeo brothers, who had been responsible for Gian'Pietro Gaffori's death, was razed to the ground after the traitors had been broken on the wheel. That it has never been rebuilt even though 220 years have elapsed since the assassination, is typical of the Corsicans' long memory.

Apart from a statue on the Place Paoli, unveiled in 1854, Pasquale's memory is perpetuated by the *Palais National,* on the southern face of the Place du Poilu, now a museum and library, closed for a time but lately re-opened. In Paoli's day, the building, very much more a large provincial residence than a palace, housed not only the experimental Corsican Parliament brought into existence by Paoli's Constitution, but also professors and a sprinkling of the students of the all Corsican university Pasquale had opened in 1765. 'Here' says Dorothy Carrington 'representative democracy was tried out, decades before the French and American revolutions', while the instruction in the university included the study of such writers as Voltaire, Rousseau, and Locke. When it is remembered that the professors were Franciscan monks, it can be seen that 'liberalism' was not confined to politics, and indeed the Paoli régime 'performed the unusual feat of reconciling Catholicism with revolutionary institutions and ideas'.

But to imprint the city on the inner eye, take the brief walk to the Belvedere, through a short maze of streets in which it would be easy to get lost but for the little red arrows marking the way. From this specially constructed view-point, one can look back to get an unforgettable impression of Vincentello's citadel and the compact mass of the old town. Below, and this is not a place for the sufferer from vertigo, is the rocky bed where the bright waters of the Tavignano and the Restonica meet in frantic embrace as they surge from their shadowy gorges.

Corte is the key to another of the island's unspoilt, mountain protected regions, the Niolo, an arcadian little world grown up round the Golo river basin, shielded by a sentinel ring of the island's highest peaks, best reached by the romantically known *Scala di Santa Regina* – the Stairway of the Holy Queen (of Heaven). Like the Asco, it is a region where the people still have a distinctive physical bearing, where the shepherd still finds a niche in life, and where also much of Corsica's most colourful folklore is rooted.

Many of the Niolons are tall and blond. They like to insist, therefore, that they, not the Corbarans, are the true Corsicans, being one with the North African Berbers who inhabited Morocco many centuries before the proselytizing hordes of the followers of the Prophet began their sweep to the west. It is always a possibility, for of the isolation of individual valley communities the Niolo is the supreme example.

The *Scala di Santa Regina* gorge is even more claustrophobic than that of the Asco, and once one has reached the Niolo plateau, the sense of a mini-cosmos is complete. The impression of height in any landscape depends largely on contrast and conflicting levels and angles, and in the Niolo, the peaks and slopes of Monte Cinto, Paglia Orba, Tafonato and the Cinque Frati, rise so abruptly that it is almost as if one were staring upwards from the bottom of a deep well. For this very reason there is something of Kashmir about Calacuccia, a large village of 1200 inhabitants, in the heart of a vast bouquet of chestnut trees; a village of medieval aspect, famous for a vendetta story, that of Maria Felice, which again proves that if women occupied a social back seat theoretically, their behind-the-scenes influence was probably considerably greater than that of their present-day emancipated sisters.

Maria was engaged to a handsome young shepherd at the time when her dearly-loved brother, a priest, was murdered. Heartbroken, she composed a superb *voceru* for the funeral, a lament for the dead and a call for vengeance. Traditionally it was the fiancé's duty to see that blood was repaid with blood, but the young shepherd not being of a combative nature was not at all anxious to expose himself to the risk of retaliation for the rest of his life. Ignoring the call, he left with his flock for distant pastures. But tradition is not easily rejected; especially in the Niolo. Overwhelmed by doubts and remorse, he returned to Calacuccia only to find a crowd gathered outside the Felice home. It was for Maria's funeral. Shame, grief, despair, a sense of unrequited love, had caused her 'to go into a decline'. In the manner of the hero of a Verdian opera, the shepherd committed suicide on her grave.

Like that of Asco, however, the Niolo's isolation is becoming a thing of the past. The hand of modernization shows itself in the form of a barrage constructed in 1968, known as the Calacuccia Lake of 25,000,000 cubic metres capacity, its role irrigation and the supply of power for the eastern plain region of Mariana.

Three kilometres from Calacuccia, on the lake shore, is the smaller village of Casamaccioli, also surrounded by giant chestnut trees, noted for its annual *fête* from the 8-10 September, festival of the Nativity of the Virgin Mary. Unlike Provence – and especially the Var – where every village, however tiny, holds its yearly *fête*, such rural festivities are rare in Corsica, so that the gathering at Casamaccioli is an important date for the whole neighbourhood.

The celebrations are always inaugurated by an open-air Mass beside a statue of the Virgin, Santa Maria della Stella, so called by reason of the little stars adorning the crown. After the blessing and the *'Ite. Missa est'*, the statue is carried to the fairground and set up for the *Granitola* (snail), a peculiar ritual, half dance, half procession, in which the congregation swelled by a number of people who have not assisted at the Mass, form a double line to begin a circling movement round the statue, curling inwards ever more tightly like a coiling snake, till the ring is finally closed. There follows a brief, silent pause, a further blessing, and the procession breaks up, still silent, in little groups.

It is at this gathering that local arts, so rapidly dying out, still cling stubbornly to life. The vocal duels – *chiama e rispondi* – together with competitions for extempore verse, are organized, and Casamaccioli is renowned island-wide for the quality of its *voceratrice*, though they, too, are a dying race; old women with sad faces and long memories. What is most likely to preserve this fête is its commercial importance. It is the meeting place for shepherds, owners of their own flocks – though they, too, are rapidly diminishing in numbers – and for local farmers, to discuss prices and prospects. The date is a convenient one for the shepherds as September is the only month in the year they can spend with wives and families. Even those with substantial homes are obliged to pass most of the year on that picturesque migration, the *transhumance,* or in the bleak discomfort of isolated *bergeries*. It is indeed a hard life. Apart from enduring living conditions one would have thought inconceivable in this day and age, there is the intense loneliness of long separations from wives and children, for whereas most nomadic communities share the pastoral life, Niolo wives stay at home, looking after crops, cultivating vegetables, caring for the livestock, and weaving. Only the fact that to be owner of a flock can still ensure a comparative financial security and a satisfactory standard of living, keeps the resolute few from drifting to the cities of the island or 'the continent'.

One can understand that with money in their pockets, the shepherds are enthusiastic supporters of the fair's gambling booths, ad hoc roulette tables, and privately organized baccarat parties, where considerable sums of money change hands, and which are so much a feature of the three days, while at the same time vast quantities of *pastis* are consumed and the shepherds for a brief moment can put sheep out of their minds.

Some idea of a shepherd's lonely life can be gained by trekking deeper into the wild interior, to the most beautiful of Corsica's natural lakes set high in the mountains, the Lac de Nino, 6000 feet above sea level, and womb of the Tavignano river.

It is not an easy walk. The track winds over and round, smooth slippery boulders, steeply upwards through a maze of decaying pines, victims of that scourge of all forests, the goat. Once the lake is reached there is a welcome stretch of flat ground, a vivid green plateau, meadow covered, in whose centre is the mirror-surfaced water. Attractive as it appears after a long climb under a fierce sun, withstand the temptation of a swim for the water is glacial and weeds grow in profusion. It is, however, the home of delicious, though small, trout.

The Plateau is one of the favourite resting places and grazing lands for the Niolo shepherds, and the countryside dotted with stone *bergeries*. Many years ago, a family passing this way hoping to reach the west coast unseen, did not have either the time or the inclination to admire the scenery. In May 1769, Carlo Bonaparte, then an ardent Paolist, and his wife Laetitia, six months pregnant with the future Emperor Napoleon, were fleeing from Corte before the advance of the French troops. It can be claimed as a miracle that the embryo Emperor ever came alive into the world. The French were hard on their heels, and all day Laetitia was being mercilessly jolted by the little mountain pony she was riding, as it slipped and stumbled over the rough tracks. Fording the Liamone, swollen by melting snows the pony swerved into deep water and was swept downstream. Carlo shouted to her to let go of the reins and make for the bank, but realising that without the mount they would never be able to complete the journey, she hung on, and by a mixture of will power and physical strength, was able to help the pony to fight his way out of the current, dragging her with him.

It was in fact, largely due to this traumatic experience that Carlo Bonaparte produced his highly practical, if somewhat cynical, remark – 'I have been a good patriot and Paolist at heart so long as the national government existed, but it exists no longer. So lets all be French! *Evviva il Re e suo governo!*' ('Long live the King and his government.')

Spreading to the north west of the Lac de Nino, is the Valdo-Niello forest already mentioned, rival in beauty to that of Aitone from which it is separated by the Col de Vergio. Valdo-Niello, means the 'dark forest', and is supposed to have given its name to that of the whole region – Niolo – since at one time its sombre ocean of trees swamped the entire valley. Always intensely xenophobic, the people of Niolo could not bring themselves to admit the finality of the Porto Novo defeat, and it was from the depths of the forest, five years later in 1774, that Tomaso Cervioni assembled a band of patriots to challenge French rule.

Unfortunately for them, French counter-intelligence was efficient. Tomaso's small force was anticipated, surrounded, and obliged to surrender, after which the French Governor, de Marbeuf, decided to make an example of the Niolo *pour encourager les autres*. A punitive expedition under General de Sionville marched into the Niolo laying waste to everything on its way. Villagers were hanged indiscriminately or tortured if they withheld information. De Sionville was reported to have an unerring eye when it came to estimating the number of hanged a branch of a tree would be able to support. Many were deported and sent to the infamous *'bagnes'* of Toulon, a fate which without exaggeration may be said to have been worse than death.

10 Bastia

Les pieds sur terre et les mains at travail

The Genoese were an industrious, thorough people, and the Genoese centre of Corsica for close on six centuries, Bastia, bears the indelible mark of the Genoese character. It is certainly the most Italianate of Corsican towns, and one can only echo Lear's opinion that it 'gives one the impression of having suddenly arrived at Leghorn or Naples'. Today, inevitably, Bastia and its region lead the social and economic revolution threatening the old order of tradition. It is from Bastia that nascent industry stretches its tentacles. Its citizens rather than orientating themselves on history, look to the future. It is also safe to say that without Genoa, there would never have been a Bastia.

In 1380, the Genoese Governor Leonello Lomellino, having been driven from his Headquarters in Biguglia by Arrigo della Rocca's patriots, decided that the tiny fishing hamlet of Cardo at the foot of Cap Corse, was the ideal site for a citadel which could both guard Cardo harbour and keep watch on the land approaches and Tuscany Straits. From the massive *bastiglia,* or keep, constructed on the cliff, the future town and Genoese capital of Corsica took its name.

Successive governors enlarged and embellished the city which soon became – and still is, for that matter – the largest on the island. In the mid-fifteenth century, the Governor Tomasino de Campofregoso, surrounded the residential and commercial areas with ramparts, at the same time inaugurating work on the citadel one sees today, and which took forty-one years (1480-1521) to complete. Yet despite these elaborate fortifications, and the fact that the city was the seat of Genoese authority, Bastia was never able to hold out, as did Calvi and Bonifacio, against determined attack.

With its history as the heart of foreign rule, the French selected Bastia as their centre when they first installed themselves on the island, using it as the main base from which they probed into the interior, and for the same reason, in reverse, it never occurred to either Paoli or Napoleon, to contemplate it as their capital. The Convention, it may be remembered, decreed that Corsica be divided into two administrative areas, Liamone and Golo, their *Chef-lieus* respectively Ajaccio and Bastia, an arrangement suppressed by Napoleon in 1811, thereby making Ajaccio the undisputed metropolis.

Today Bastia counts 51,000 inhabitants as against Ajaccio's 38,700, and this numerical superiority is likely to increase by reason of the former's rapid development. There is even talk of reviving the Covention's decree in view of Bastia's growing economic predominance. Furthermore, this once most Italian of cities has redeemed herself in the eyes of chauvinistic islanders, by the fact that it was the centre of the *maquis* during the Italo-German occupation, suffered severely during the fighting in September and October 1943, and was honoured with the *Croix de Guerre* by General de Gaulle 'in recognition of the courage and spirit of resistance of its inhabitants'.

Corsica, as we have seen, has never been renowned for its works of art. The successive cultural waves influencing Europe swept past the island, so that ideas were late and imported, till recently almost exclusively from Italy, initially making their influence felt in Bastia, which for this reason holds pride of place in ecclesiastical art. Largest of the city's many churches, presenting a most impressive facade, is that of Saint John the Baptist, whose twin towers overlook the *Vieux Port,* a comparatively recent construction dating back to 1640. Ornate, ebulliently Italian in style, the interior is a confusion of gilded stucco and gleaming marble. More rewarding are the two 'chapels' that of the Conception and of Saint Roch.

Though again comparatively modern, the *Chapelle de la Conception* has a Murillo over the high altar, a grandiose statute of the Immaculate Conception to the left of the pulpit, and an eighteenth-century Genoese cross. What is unique, both here and in the Chapel de Saint Roch, built by a rival fraternity, is the incredible richness of the interior decoration. In its attempt to outdo the rival chapel in splendour, the walls of *La Conception* are panelled with red damask, while magnificent chandeliers hang from the vaulted, painted ceiling. Since no other building in Corsica could stand comparison with so regal a *décor,* the French decided to use it for the assemblies of the Corsican *Etats,* and later, Sir Gilbert Elliott, equally impressed, preferred it to the Governor's Palace for the first meeting of the newly constituted Anglo-Corsican Parliament – a most stormy affair – in February 1795.

Although severely damaged in the 1943 fighting, the old *Palais des Gouverneurs* is still the principal edifice of the citadel, the solid round tower which forms its right-angle and corner of the south wall being the original *bastiglia* which gave the city its name. The Germans deliberately blew up much of the building in the course of their last battle, and the old Bastia museum is now being replaced by the *Musée d'Ethnographie Corse,* devoted to all aspects of island life, recalling in its scope Arles' Musée Arleten. The varied collection is being constantly added to, and will soon be endowed with a new hall in which paintings from the great Fesch collection will be hung, while the island's classical past is recalled by the *Centre de Documentation d'Archeologie sous-marine* and Roman *amphorae* recovered from the many wrecks resting on the sea bed off the dangerous coast.

To the right of the museum is a memorial, to remind one of the 'continent's' debt to the island, to the essentially Corsican 173rd and 373rd infantry regiments, which played so important a part in the battles of Verdun and Saint Quentin in the First World War, and on the Aisne in 1940. Nearby is another curious relic, the turret of the submarine *Casabianca,* one of the escapees from Toulon harbour in November 1942 when as a reprisal for the allied invasion of North Africa, the

Germans overran Vichy France. Most of the French fleet lying at anchor was scuttled on the orders of Admiral Laborde, who though definitely anglophobe, was not prepared to let his ships fall into German hands. The *Casabianca,* however, managed to make her way to Algiers, and from then on under the command of *Capitaine de vaisseau* Lherminier, acted as liaison between the island's resistance movement and Free French HQ in North Africa. The story goes back further however, for the *Casabianca* was named after the young Corsican hero, the twelve-year-old Jacques de Casabianca of 'The boy stood on the burning deck' fame.

In 1798, Jacques sailed for Egypt on the frigate commanded by his father, Louis de Casabianca. On 10 August the British and French fleets met in the battle of the Nile – or Aboukir Bay. Louis, who had issued the strictest orders that no matter what the circumstances every man should remain at his post, was killed in the early stages, and not long after his death, caught by the concentrated broadsides of the British fleet, the frigate was blazing from bows to stern. The crew abandoned ship, but Jacques, faithful to his father's orders, remained, alone, on the 'burning deck' till the vessel, *L'Orient,* blew up as flames reached the powder hold.

L'Eglise de Sainte Marie dates from 1495, but was restored in 1604 and again in 1938. Originally the cathedral of the Bishop of Mariana, it seems to have lapsed from its pride of place after the consecration of the Church of Saint John the Baptist. It is worth visiting to see a silver group, the Assumption of the Virgin, an eighteenth-century work, most delicately executed, and which is carried through the streets in procession on 15 August, day of the Feast of the Assumption. The painting on wood, representing the Assumption, was one might say 'looted' from the more ancient church of La Canonica which will be mentioned later; the artist is unknown but the date 1512.

The *Chapelle Sainte-Croix,* on the far side of the Rue de l'Evêché owes its name to a black crucifix, generally known as *Le Christ des Miracles.* In 1428, according to legend, anchovy fishermen plying their trade by night, saw a strange light out to sea. This was found to be the black cross, with the figure of the nailed Christ, now in the church. The fishermen immediately took their find to the chapel belonging to the monks of the Brotherhood of the Annunciation, who were so amazed by the discovery that their chapel was immediately renamed that of the *Sainte-Croix*. Every year anchovy fishermen offer their first catch of the season to the Brotherhood. Like the Chapel of the Conception, the interior is a blaze of guilt stucco, dating from the time of Louis XV, to such an extent that one hears complaints that is is more like an old-fashioned opera house than a place of worship. This riot of ornamentation rather overawes the beautiful painting of the *Vierge de l'Annonciation* which adorns the high altar, a work of the sixteenth-century Florentine, Filiberto.

In the citadel's centre, off the rue du Dragon, is the Place Guasco. This is named after Charles Fortuné Guasco, born in Bastia in 1826, a talented but comparatively unrecognized artist, one of whose paintings – Pericles weeping over the corpse of his son dead from plague – is hung in the Museum. It is a little confusing that there was a bishop Ignace Guasco, who, in 1791, was driven from his See by a band of women.

In the eyes of the devout Bastia housewives, led by a formidable amazon, Flora Oliva, popularly known as *'La Colonelle'*, the Bishop had committed a mortal sin in agreeing to the new revolutionary laws of France which brought the church under temporal control. Worked up to a frenzy by *'La Colonelle's'* oratory, they invaded the episcopal palace, and obliged the bewildered bishop to take the first boat sailing for Italy.

Old travelogues and guide books always advised a tour of the *Vieux Port* and an evening stroll along the *Jetée du Dragon*, in order to appreciate the atmosphere of the old town and obtain a general view of the citadel. This particular quarter of Bastia was not so much specifically Corsican, as typically Mediterranean. Lear mentions Naples and Leghorn (Livorno). He could just as well have quoted Marseille's *vieux port* prior to its destruction by the Germans, or old Nice; the sheer multi-storeyed buildings hung with drying,

highly-colourful underwear, and the dark *'bistrots'* where 'wine is the only drink served . . . and where one meets types truly representative of the quarter and hears them exhanging views on any subject from town gossip to the latest international crisis '. But not any more! In the stampede to modernize, the old town is due to be demolished, its colourful houses replaced by soulless *immeubles,* possibly an improvement from the strictly hygienic point of view; aesthetically a disaster.

Till the upsurge of fashionable Calvi, Bastia was undoubtedly the most animated of Corsica's cities, the centre of island cultural life. In 1794, Samuel Rice, a young subaltern of the 51st, wrote 'it (Bastia) is a large and populous place, and resembles very much the generality of French towns. We are going to be very gay here. An Italian opera is shortly to open, which is to be patronized by the Governor and is much approved of by the garrison. A coffee house for English papers is also to be established, a much better thing than the former. In fact, you do not know how grand we are going to be.'

An opera house was indeed built but not opened, as far as I can discover, till 1873, when the impressive building, small scale copy of Milan's La Scala, echoed to the strains of Verdi's *Rigoletto.* A very popular institution. the theatre was unfortunately heavily damaged in October 1943. I find it strange that it has not been rebuilt, especially in a city where the human voice is so appreciated. In fact one of the streets is named after the great Corsican tenor, César Vezzani, whose voice at its best had a truly Caruso-like ring.

Any one who appreciates bustle should not leave Bastia without taking an evening *apéritif* on the terrace of one of the many cafés on the huge Place Saint Nicholas, the hub of city life. Many have their own little orchestra, those that do not, are mostly equipped with juke boxes. In the evening when offices have closed, and the *place* is given over to the *passegiata,* the ritual youth parade, the noise is great, but most people seem to enjoy it.

The *place* is graced by a white marble statue of *L'Empereur,* again in Roman garb, work of the Florentine Bartolini. But the one-time arbiter of continental Europe does not seem

24 PROPRIANO, modern tourist centre

happy in these surroundings. Hardly surprising, perhaps, since it was he who stripped Bastia of the predominant role she had played for so many centuries.

Bastia is certainly the best base for a tour of Cap Corse, that slender northern finger of the island, forty kilometres long and fifteen kilometres at its widest, an area which possesses a marked individuality. In Cap Corse it is the sea rather than the mountains which imposes itself, and its inhabitants, turning their eyes to the outside world, are considered the most un-Corsican of Corsicans, seldom inspired in the past by that fanatical nationalism, hallmark of the island character. It is one of the richer areas, since the people have a double source of income; the fruits of the sea and those of the soil. For while the men fish, the women exploit the land which is a natural garden; orchards, vineyards, olive groves.

If any part of Corsica can be said to have suffered Genoa gladly, then it was Cap Corse, feudal till well into the eighteenth century, fief of two great families, the Mare in the north, the Gentile in the south. Their passivity *vis-à-vis* the national cause was encouraged by the grant of privileges by the invader, but, nevertheless, there were times when Corsican blood asserted itself above mere material interests, and a Jacques (Giacomo) de Mare was at Sampiero's side the day he was lured into the fatal ambush laid by the Ornano brothers.

The grand tour of the Cap, from Bastia to Saint Florent, can easily be accomplished in a day, but involves so much and such variety of interest, that an overnight halt is strongly recommended.

Starting up the east coast from Bastia, one comes to the church of Notre Dame de Lavasina, a noted pilgrimage site on the occasion of the feast of the Nativity of the Virgin Mary; 8 September. The tiny church in addition to a superb painting *La Madone de Lavasina*, by an artist of the Perugino school, and a marble altar said to have been taken from a monastery from the Tuscan town of Pistoja, is remarkable for the mass of ex-votos which smother its walls, expressing gratitude to Our Lady for miraculous escapes from death, and recovery from serious maladies.

Two and a half kilometres up the coast, the village of Erbalunga, its houses grouped on a rocky promontory, is sometimes called the Corsican Collioure. Architecturally, this is something of a exaggeration, but for lovers of the sea it is a delightful spot, conforming to that popular French expression, *les pieds dans l'eau,* and where the inhabitants boast they can fish for whitebait from their windows. It is the birthplace of the author Paul Valéry, born at the moment of France's prostration in 1871, dying at the moment of the allied triumph in 1945, and of the great *maître-avocat,* Moro-Giafferi, the Edward Carson of the French law courts of the twenties. From the little town one can look up to the peak of Monte Stello, 4200 feet, the highest point of Cap Corse, a favourite climb for anyone wishing to enjoy a vast panorama of sea and mountain, and yet avoid the killing fatigue involved in the ascent of the central summits.

The *Marine de Sisco* stands at the opening of the Sisco valley, a little *commune* which affords another example of the ravages of depopulation. In the eighteenth century it was one of the island's most prosperous. Local industries flourished – the fabrication of jewellery, weaving of cloth, lace-making, even a little arms factory – providing ample employment and a living wage for the inhabitants of its seventeen hamlets. But today the entire area boasts only 508 survivors of this golden age, those who still prefer a simple life in a setting of shady chestnut trees and sweet-smelling shrubs to the luxuries and petrol fumes of the city.

On reaching Macinaggio, singled out for development as a *port de plaisance,* which it is hoped will bring back a measure of prosperity to a once rich but now depressed area, the coastal road turns inland, over the col Saint Nicolas to Ersa, through the Rogliano *commune,* today counting a bare 560 inhabitants, in 1646 a thriving community of over 4000 souls.

The scheme of making Macinaggio a pleasure resort should succeed. It is an ideal spot for a beach holiday. The climate is mild, the scenery relaxing and gentle, in contrast with the stern grandeur which is so typical of the rest of the island.

It was from Macinaggio, also, that the only 'combined operation' in Corsican military history was launched.

It will be remembered that one of Pasquale Paoli's ambitions was to create a patriot fleet. In 1757, he established a shipyard at Centuri on the western coast, exactly opposite Macinaggio then one of the few places on the Cap still in Genoese hands. Thanks to enthusiastic, unremitting, toil, the Corsicans had soon produced fourteen medium-sized vessels, firm basis for the future fleet. In 1761, Macinaggio itself fell to Paoli, who immediately converted the little port into a naval base for operations against the sea lanes between Genoa and Bastia. Paoli realised that the threat to this vital communication would be even greater if he could seize the nearby island of Capraja – separated by forty kilometres of sea from Macinaggio – and wipe out or neutralize the Genoese garrison. It would, as he put it, cut 'the umbilical cord which binds the Most Serene Republic to what is left of its colony'.

The expedition, however, did not get under way till the 16 February 1767. Though tardy, it was completely successful. Commanded by Paoli's friend, the talented Achille Murati, the attackers landed unopposed, and before the Genoese had time to recover from their surprise, they found themselves besieged in their citadel of the Bay of Ceppo. Nevertheless they resisted desperately, unable to believe that the puny Corsican fleet would be able to hold off the relief force they felt was bound to be sent. They were mistaken. Several attemps by a Genoese flotilla to raise the siege were defeated, and the only Genoese who did manage to land on 3 May, were wiped out within a few hours. Eventually, on 31 May, the Genoese commander, Bernardo Ottone, raised the white flag, and signed a document of formal surrender. The Corsicans had scored a victory, small from a purely military standpoint, but of immense importance politically, and Voltaire wrote enthusiastically *'C'est plutôt aux Corses à conquerir Pise et Gênes qu'à Gênes et Pise subjuguer les Corses'* ('It is now more appropriate for the Corsicans to conquer the Pisans and the Genoese, than for Genoa and Pisa to subjugate Corsica'). Later Napoleon, commenting on the expedition, paid Murati the compliment of saying *'Il n'a manque à Murati qu'n théâtre plus vaste pour être un autre Turenne'*. (Murati only needed a wider field of operations to became a second Turenne.)

Macinaggio was the scene of Paoli's disembarkation on his native soil in 1790 after twenty five years exile, spent mostly in London, and also that of Napoleon, on 10 May, 1793, after his flight from Ajaccio, and prior to his abortive attempt to persuade Bastia to renounce Paoli and remain faithful to France. In 1869, on her return from Egypt after the opening of the Suez Canal, the Empress Eugenie, tired after the strenuous round of ceremonies at which most of Europe's crowned heads or highest ranking representatives had assisted, landed briefly before continuing on the last lap of the voyage, since when part of the road from the port to Rogliano has been known as *Le Chemin de l'Impératrice*.

To Centuri it is only eighteen kilometres by direct route, a continuation of the peripheral N198, with a brief loop, after passing the Bocca di Serra, and the *moulin Mattei* (another spectacular view-point) adding an extra five kilometres to the journey. It is worth while, for Centuri, with its neat white houses and their green-tiled roofs, miniature harbour, the pinky sands of its small *plage,* is utterly unspoilt and there – if you can afford it – you get the best *langouste* on the island.

Cap Corse's western coast conforms with the general physical pattern. It is more picturesque than the east, more wooded, more dramatic. The mountains, or hills as they are here, rise more steeply from the shore; the majority of the villages resemble gigantic eagles' nests on their granite crags; and most impressive of all, the most *perché* of all *villages perchés*, is the astonishing Nonza on its great dark rock, crowned by a fortified tower. Many of its houses seem to sprout from the cliffs which serve as their foundation. It was here that the young Carthaginian, Julie refused to abjure her faith. There is an *'image d'Epinal'* depicting her martyrdom, a remarkable mixture of conventional stylisation and realism. Julie is shown tied to an olive tree, her left hand raised at an angle of forty-five degrees, the right by her side; stripped to the waist blood drips from her (still intact) breasts. Her head is framed by a halo so thick that it hides part of the tree trunk, while the expression on her face is, to say the least, wooden. On the other hand, the executioner's features betray a most vivid brutality. Beneath close cropped hair, separated from bushy eyebrows by a low forehead, his eyes glow as he opens a pair of giant, serrated pincers. He is obviously about to begin the horrible torture, and looking forward to so doing. The little springs at the foot of the cliff are generally said to have gushed miraculously as the severed breasts fell on the rocks, and to contain healing powers. Yet one of the latest guide books chooses to ignore the legend, merely stating when referring to the village church of Sainte Julie, that it recalls the martyrdom of 'this young Christian of Nonza who was crucified under Diocletian in 303'.

In more modern times, Nonza became famous at the time of the Paoli saga. Determined to subdue Corsican resistance, the French launched a three-pronged attack from the Bastia region in the summer of 1768. One column, commanded by General Grandmaison, about 1200 strong, was given Nonza as its first objective. Though an immensely strong natural position, the Corsican general, Barbaggi, was afraid to risk having his main force shut up inside the walls, and decided to fall back north to retain his power of manoeuvre. One of Nonza's garrison was an old soldier, Jacques (Giacomo) Casella, still suffering from a wound obliging him to use crutches. Pointing out that he would only be a burden to a mobile force, he begged Barbaggi to let him stay behind and do what he could to hold up the enemy advance, if only for a few minutes.

Next day the leading detachments of de Grandmaison's column began to close in on the village. No sooner were they within range than they were met by a well aimed fire from every loophole on the battlements. There were a number of casualties. The advance was halted, and the French soldiers hastily took cover. Studying the position, and impressed by the accuracy of the fire which greeted every hint of forward movement, Grandmaison came to the conclusion that an all out assault would prove highly costly and sent an envoy under the protection of a white flag to try to arrange a capitulation. The envoy eventually returned with a message which had been dropped from the ramparts that the Governor of the Tower made it known that – 'The Corsican garrison agrees to leave the fort if it does so with its banner flying, with its arms and equipment, and accorded full military honours. Furthermore the French must agree to furnish the necessary transport to enable it to rejoin the bulk of the national army'.

They were stiff terms, but de Grandmaison accepted, ordering his men to form up as if on parade before the main gate, and present arms. 'The gate opened, and out came a little old man on crutches which he was trying to give a certain martial rhythm.'

When nobody else appeared, the astonished – and slightly suspicious – de Grandmaison asked where the rest of the garrison was hiding.

'In my person, Monsieur le General' was the reply 'you see both Governor and Garrison!'

For a moment, so it is said, the French general believed he must be in the presence of the Devil himself, especially as it was popularly held that Satan suffered from a permanent limp, but at last old Casella was able to persuade de Grandmaison that he had successfully sustained the role of a one man army by sighting a musket at each loophole, and running from the one to the other, firing and reloading, as fast as his crutches would allow. In 1768, the age of chivalry had not died. De Grandmaison was a big enough man to appreicate his enemy's courage, and to be able to laugh at himself. Not only did he stick to the terms of the treaty he had been fooled into signing, but he sent Casella back to Murato, Paoli's headquarters, with an escort of cavalry to protect him against the possible dangers of the road.

At the extreme western foot of the Cap, in a frame of vineyards, olive groves and orchards, is the little town of Saint Florent which has always played a leading part in Corsican history, today with a population of only just over 800. Founded by the Genoese, and inevitably endowed with a citadel in the late fifteenth century, it is now a very popular summer resort.

As a port from which Calvi could be either neutralized or threatened directly, Saint Florent, or San Fiorenzo, as it was originally called, was constantly changing hands in the course of the Genoese wars. In the late eighteenth century British naval strategy was of the opinion that its sheltered deep-water harbour would make a convenient base from which to counter moves by the French fleet based on Toulon. This major consideration undoubtedly helped to bring the negotiations engaged between Britain and Paoli's independent Corsica to a satisfactory conclusion, and lead to Saint Florent being the objective of the first major operation undertaken by British forces on Corsican soil.

On 7 February 1794, five British men-of-war, *Alcide, Egmont, Fortitude, Juno,* and *Victory,* sailed into the Gulf of Saint Florent and anchored off Punta Martella, so called because of the Martello tower protecting the headland sheltering the harbour, and that same evening landed a mixed army and naval force of 700 men and thirty-two cannon. The initial attack failed, but when the tower came under the concentrated fire of the English ships, its commander surrendered. On 17 February, Colonel Moore's 51st of Foot and the Royals, stormed the redoubt the French had christened the *Convention,* and on the 19 February the remainder of the Saint Florent garrison surrendered. With the return of peace at the end of the Napoleonic wars, and in the evolving world France and Britain becoming allies instead of eternal enemies and rivals, Saint Florent, overshadowed by Calvi and Ile Rousse, seemed to lose its *raison d'être,* and as a consequence slipped into a slow decline. In the twenties, it was described as 'a sad little town', and a further gloomy note – 'The harbour at the head of the large and beautiful bay, capable of being a fine port, is depressing in its desolation'.

But once again the discovery of the sun has rejuvenated the town, as it has so many other decaying island resorts. Today it could never for a moment be qualified as either 'sad' or 'depressing'. There cannot be many places of only 800 inhabitants which can boast seven first-class hotels, many excellent restaurants, and three camping sites, one of them *U Pezzo,* reckoned by some to be the best on the island. Much the same may also be said of the region, the Nebbio, on whose northern fringe it stands. Formerly looked upon as unhealthy, impossible to live in past mid-April, it is now highly popular with those who want to enjoy the sun but avoid the crowds.

The Nebbio, long before Saint Florent came into being, was one of the ancient bishoprics of Corsica, and a major attraction for the tourist is the fact that so many of the early Pisan churches are to be found still in comparatively good state of repair, amongst them the former Nebbio cathedral, the church of Oletta, and that of San Michele near Murato.

It is only a matter of minutes to reach the cathedral on foot from Saint Florent and it is again a sad reflection on vandalism so that its doors have to be kept shut, so that one has to ask for the key at the *Auberge d'Europe* on the *Place des Portes*, near the war memorial. Today, the cathedral is the only vestige of what was probably an impressive city; ancient Nebbio, abandoned by the living in the sixteenth century.

Compared with such gems as Saint Trophime in Arles or the Basilica of Saint Mary Magdalene at Saint Maximim, the cathedral's facade is almost frighteningly severe, with its three unadorned lesser, superimposed on five huge blind arcades with crudely decorated capitals. The lintel of the stark door has a faint motif of shells and crockets, while in the arch of each of the flanking arcades is a porthole-style window set in a square stone plaque. In the central arcade above the lintel, is the only figure carving to relieve the general puritanical aspect, that of the Virgin holding the infant Jesus in her arms. The interior design is that of the majority of early Mediterranean churches, three timber roofed naves, again strictly plain. According to one's personal leanings such austerity may be considered either admirable or to be regretted. In the oven-shaped apse, however, is a gilded statue carved in wood of Saint Flor, a Roman soldier who preferred to die rather than forswear his new-found faith, and whose relics are in the glass coffer to the right. The white marble statue of the Virgin was the gift of one of the famous Dorias,

Giovanni. Saint Flor's relics were originally placed in the Roman catacombs, but later offered as a gift to Monsignor Guasco, Bishop of Nebbio.

The simple tomb is that of the highly controversial figure, General Gentile. An ardent Paolist in his youth, he turned against the *Babbu della Patria,* when after the latter's quarrel with the revolutionary French government, he called in the British. From then on Gentile became an equally ardent Bonapartist. Napoleon made him a general in 1796, but two years later, before able to take part in any of the more famous of the Napoleonic campaigns, he died at the age of 47.

The road to Oletta lies through the heart of the rich Nebbio country, which has much of the pastoral quality of the Niolo, but without the latter's brooding isolation. It is a friendly, smiling, landscape, totally relaxing, striking a happy medium between the brittle overcrowded coast, and the savage, introspective Niolo and Sartenais; the deep south. These pleasant orchards, bright torrents and lush fields, make it difficult to understand the meaning of the word *vendetta!* It is worth climbing Oletta hill – the place itself is an overgrown village with a bigger permanent population than Saint Florent – to visit the church and its very beautiful triptych, a primitive in the better sense of the word, the central panel, the Virgin suckling the infant, framed by Saint Reparata and Saint Andrew. For another very much less spiritual reason, I advise a halt in Oletta, in order to have a meal of fresh *pain de campagne* and local cheese, a blue which some will find an excellent substitute for roquefort, and others may even dare to compare with stilton.

Three kilometres further on, in the Bastia direction, is the tiny village of Olmeta-di-Tuda, almost surrounded by a dense cluster of huge elms, a rarity in Corsica, with a nineteenth-century castle, that of Marshal Count Horace François Bastien Sebastiani, one of the most colourful of Napoleon's marshals, a *beau sabreur,* and reported to have been the handsomest man in the Empire. Born in 1773 at La Porta d'Ampugnano, he was with the young Bonaparte in Italy at Arcola and Verona. For a short time ambassador to Turkey, he claimed to have circumvented a British attempt to get control of the Bosphorus. Back in France, he was with Napoleon in almost every campaign. He fought the British in Portugal and Spain, and was one of the fortunate survivors of the horrors of the retreat from Moscow. Like other Napoleonic heroes, he rallied to the cause of the Bourbons after Waterloo. Louis Philippe made him Minister of Foreign Affairs. He died in Paris in 1851, at the age of 79, having lived to see the nephew of his friend and benefactor crowned Emperor Napoleon III.

From Olmeta, a sharp climb of a kilometre brings one to the Bocca (or col) di San Stefano, where a minor road forks sharp right to Murato, and the famous church of San Michele, but again for the visit one has to find the *Curé* of Murato and persuade him of one's *bona fides*.

Though close to the village, the church gives an impression of isolation, situated on a promontory, surrounded by meadows with a single rather sad tree as its sole companion. Built about 1150, like the church at Aregno, its walls present a chess board pattern of curiously intermingled green and white stone, taken from the nearby Bevinco river. The original lines, have been upset by the superimposition of a clock tower supported on two squat stone blocks, which gives it a strangely hybrid aspect. The interior after the style of a miniature Nebbio cathedral, is more interesting than that of its larger sister. The typical Romanesque 'loophole' windows are framed in blocks decorated with highly imaginative carvings; the Temptation of Eve by the serpent, and the eternal struggle between good and evil, interpreted by two intertwined snakes attempting to hypnotize two birds of indeterminate species. The arch of the apse must also have been rich in frescos, but the passing of centuries has left only vague traces, though it is thought the principal motif was that of the Annunciation.

as his HQ by Paoli in his last campaign of 1768-69, is locally renowned as the birthplace of a man named Fieschi who, in July 1835, threw an 'infernal machine' at Louis-Philippe. The monarch was unharmed, but the explosion killed and injured a number of Parisians in the vicinity, including the Napoleonic veteran, Marshal Mortier, Duc de Trevise. Fieschi was arrested and executed the following year. There is nothing of great interest in Murato village itself, except for a painting of Saint Mary Magdalene above the church's high altar which many claim, though there is no proof, to be an original Titian.

From Murato, one can return to the west coast and Ile Rousse, by the village of Pieve and the hilly road through San-Pietro-di-Tenda with its sprawling hillside village and, just beyond, the ruins of an unusually large Romanesque church, once the chapel of the abandoned Franciscan monastery one sees to the right of the road. It is a pity that no money has been provided for the chapel's restoration, for what one can still see of the frescos give the impression that they must have been unique of their kind; garish human masks, heads of animals and birds, flowers, purely geometric designs.

In places the road is little better than a track till the N199 is reached. There one turns left to cross the *Desert des Agriates,* yet another example of the amazing contrasts to be found in so comparatively restricted an area as Corsica. For whereas the general impression taken away by any visitor is of trees, meadows, orchards, bright waters, an overall rich green, this particular area of 40,000 acres is totally uncultivated and uninhabited, the only sign of life an occasional *bergerie,* occupied only in winter, a stretch of stony, rocky, waste land, reminiscent in some ways of the Crau, that semi-desert between the Carmargue and Marseille, scene of Mireille's fatal escapade in search on her beloved Vincent, in Mistral's epic poem of the same name. Grey and mournful, the Agriates desert only takes on a fleeting touch of colour in the spring when, as Pierre Benoit, author of *Atlantide* and *La Chatelaine du Liban,* says 'a kind of bloody carpet, from the mouth of the Aliso to that of the Ostriconi, seems to cover the Agriates from one end to the other. It is the moment of the flowering of 'fire' anemones . . . in the warm hours of the early morning, the sea breeze ripples this scarlet drapery, a red shroud whose mysteries are not yet ready to be revealed'. This indeed is one of the few places in Europe where summer heat attains an almost Saharan intensity.

11 The Cockpit of Corsica

Qui gascono u 9 maghiu 1769 e milizie di Pasquale di Paoli luttendo per a liberta di a patria – 'Here fell on 9 May 1769 the militia of Pasquale de Paoli fighting for the liberty of their country.'

The 102 kilometres between Bastia and Solenzara on the east coast, constitute Corsica's unique Plain, and largely for this reason have tended to be the background for the majority of the countless campaigns waged on Corsican soil, and the obvious beach head for seaborne invasion: Greek, Roman, Pisan, Genoese and French. Today, the plain is the solid base from which the budding industrial invasion pushes out its tentacles.

Yet till after the Second World War, this plain, with its lakes and marshes, mosquito infested, was the least populated area of the whole island; unhealthy, haunted by memories of patriot disasters. From 1957, however, SOMIVAC – *Société pour la mise en valeur agricole de la Corse* – has radically changed its present and prospects for the future by reclaiming 38,000 acres from the swamps and *maquis* which have since been so successfully cultivated that the once-abandoned region has become the symbol of the Corsica of tomorrow. The whole area is now a vast market garden and vineyard, doubled by tourist facilities which include camping sites and specially planned *sites balnéaires*. Hotels, restaurants, and *immeubles* (apartment blocks), sprout like mushrooms, and after a years' absence, a once familiar spot has become unrecognizable.

But the country between Bastia and Solenzara is still a tragic reminder of the past, of the many lives lost in the vain thousand years' struggle for liberty which, after a short but glorious moment of euphoria, was brought to a bloody end at Ponte Nuovo.

To begin with, on the Col de Teghine, only a few kilometres from Bastia is a memorial to the last battle fought on Corsican soil; in October 1943. Despite the Italian capitulation, the Germans in Corsica had decided to fight to the last and were heavily dug in on the three cols between Bastia and Saint Florent. Their final centre of resistance was the Col de Teghine stormed only after a series of furious attacks by French colonial troops, *Tirailleurs Marocains,* and *Goums,* the latter semi-irregulars, tribesmen from the Atlas Mountains who had played an important role in Italy, much dreaded by the Germans for their murderous night raids.

Returning to the main road, now the most traffic-jammed on the island, one reaches the road junction of Casamozza, where the N193 turns inland following the Golo river to Ponte-Leccia, and the coastal road to Solenzaro and eventually Bonifacio, becomes the N198. Below Casamozzo is the small town of Vescovato, capital of the Casinca region, once a bishop's see, and birthplace of the historian Filippini and the 'General of the Nation', Andrea Colonna Ceccaldi.

In June 1564, Sampiero disembarked on the west coast with a handful of men and marched on Bastia. At Vescovato, his way was barred by 1000 Genoese who, seeing that his forces numbered a bare 200, promptly attacked. The people of Vescovato, enjoying ringside seats of the battle were certain that Sampiero would be overwhelmed. Instead it was the Genoese who broke and fled. Soon afterwards the Genoese Governor, Nicola Negri, took the field with a considerably bigger army only to run into an ambush near Ponte Nuovo; 300 Genoese, including Negri, were killed, some 200 taken prisoner. 'The first fugitives who reached Bastia' says the historian Marini 'were completely stunned and couldn't even speak; they didn't know what planet they were on'.

But before reaching Casamozza, on the N193, is the village of Furiani where the war generally known as 'The Forty Years War' broke out in 1729. It was in the citadel, whose ruins dominate the village, that Luigi Giafferi, another of the 'Generals of the Nation', showed the Genoese the pattern of things to come by holding out against all attacks which he and his men repulsed with extremely heavy losses.

Three kilometres south is Biguglia, another village built commandingly along a ridge, where ancient and contemporary history mingle, for Biguglia was the site chosen, first by the Pisans, later by the Genoese, as capital of their Corsican 'colony'. It was after being driven out of Biguglia by Arrigo della Rocca, that the discomfited Genoese Governor set up his new headquarters at the little fishing village of Cardo, and ordered the construction of the *bastiglia* on the dominating cliff, from which eventually blossomed Bastia.

Branching off to the right, a secondary road, the D7, takes one to Borgo, scene of the greatest of all Patriot military triumphs.

By the Treaty of Versailles, 1764, it may be remembered, exhausted by the failure of her centuries old struggle to subdue the turbulent islanders, Genoa ceded Corsica to France, an immoral transaction since Corsica was not hers to give. Nevertheless, once the Treaty had been signed, a considerable French army landed at Bastia and in July 1768 began to push inland.

Having been unable to hold Cap Corse, Paoli decided to evacuate the Nebbio and make his major stand in the mountains, but before so doing, seeing that the French were perhaps a little over-confident, launched a surprise counter-attack which obliged the French commander, the Marquis de Chauvelin, to give ground, though leaving behind a strong garrison in Borgo village under Colonel de Ludre. By 5 October, the Corsicans had completely surrounded the village and the French were running short of food and ammunition. The Corsicans still further improved their position when, on the night of the 6/7th, a 'commando' force under Paoli's brother Clemente, seized a number of houses on the outer perimeter and the main water point.

Aware of the gravity of the situation, de Chauvelin despatched two columns to raise the siege. One under de

Grandmaison, the man who had successfully overrun Cap Corse, was halted at Oletta in an attempt to turn Paoli's flank from the north. The second and stronger of the two, including ten companies of Grenadiers under General D'Arcambal, struck directly at Borgo, and in turn surrounded the Corsicans who thus found themselves caught between two fires.

On 9 October, de Chauvelin himself arrived in person with considerable reinforcements expecting to annihilate the Patriot force, but it was at this stage that Pasquale Paoli showed that he was not, as his detractors like to suggest, totally lacking in military genius and physical courage. In a gesture worthy of Bonaparte at Lodi, he placed himself at the head of his men to lead a desperate charge on the French mass.

The struggle lasted ten hours. The French enjoyed the reputation of being the world's greatest military power, but the Corsicans were inspired by a fanatical belief in their cause. As night fell 'the troops of de Chauvelin weakened. They fell back. They broke. It was a rout. The French army was hurled back to the walls of Bastia. The soldiers of de Ludre, still encircled, mad with thirst, short of food and munitions, despairing of help, surrendered.' This shattering defeat cost the French 600 dead, 1000 wounded, six standards and nine cannon.

General Dumouriez, at the time a lieutenant, later the victor of Valmy and Jemappes, noted in his memoirs 'The Corsicans emerged with flying colours from this campaign which, lightly undertaken and badly executed ended in shame. Paoli acted boldly, his plans being well coordinated and carried out with finesse and precision. He showed genius and great strength of character and a most admirable courage.'

A diversion into the dawn of Corsican history can now be made to the ruins of Mariana and the church of La Canonica, by taking the road to the left in the direction of Bastia's airport, Poretta, to the *Auberge de la Canonica* to find the guide for a visit to the ruins, the church and the little museum. Poretta, incidentally, was the airfield from which the famous

author and aviator, Antoine de Saint Exupéry, set out for a
mission over the mainland on 31 July 1944. His total
disappearance remains one of the Second World War's
unsolved mysteries. The author of *Le Petit Prince* took off, 'his
plane was watched as it became lost in the blue of the sky, and
after that no trace of any sort!'

It was in 259 BC that the Romans first came to Corsica, but
in those leisurely days when a century could slip by on the
same changeless rhythm, it was not till 93 BC, that Marius,
renowned for his great victory over the Teuton hordes at
Pourrières near Aix-en-Provence, founded two military
colonies, the one at Mariana, the other further down the coast
at the former Greek settlement of Alalia, renamed Aleria.
These colonies were far from having a civilizing influence on
the natives, since their basic purpose was 'to rid Italy of bands
of adventurers, trouble-makers, and mutinous soldiers'. The
local tribes we are told 'could never do other than feel a bitter
hatred for the vile soldiers installed on the Fatherland'. The
opposition to Mariana, possibly because the colonists were in
an even lower category, was so great that the Romans
preferred to concentrate on the development of Aleria,
eventually to grow into a considerable city, and little detail is
known of Mariana's story except that it was several times
destroyed and rebuilt. After the fall of Rome the coast was
ravaged by Vandals, Visigoths, and the forces of Byzantium,
while rampant malaria contributed to make the surroundings
even more unhospitable; yet it was here, close to the site of a
fourth century cathedral, that the church of La Canonica was
consecrated in 1119 by the Archbishop of Pisa. Prototype of
Corsican Pisan churches, it is also the most austere in line,
relieved only by the multi-colours of the stone used in the
building, which came from the Sisco and Brando quarries.

The architectural inspiration is that of the Roman basilica;
a rectangular body divided into three naves ending with an
oven-shaped *(cul de four)* apse. The treasures the church once
held have been removed, including a primitive of the
Assumption which is now in the church of Sainte-Marie in
Bastia. The frescos of the west door, however, are unusually

animated for their period, and this has given rise to the theory that the decorators were either men of Lombardy or Pisans who had studied under Lombardian masters. Of the original cathedral, only the foundations, and the square baptistry, reminder of the days of total immersion, remain. On the baptistry floor can be seen mosaics representing 'The Four Rivers of Paradise', fishes, drinking stags, the whole conception a theme to portray the happiness of years ahead once the world's turmoil and eternal strife had become a thing of the past; happy days for which, unfortunately, we are still waiting.

Close by La Canonica – about 500 metres – is the much smaller, older church of San Parteo, but similar in general design, and noted for the harmony of its apse and the strange profane motif which decorates the south door's lintel. This shows a primitively stylized tree, flanked on either side by a lion, a motif, introduced into Europe by cloth woven with a similar pattern imported from the East, and eagerly adapted by western craftsmen as a variant to their own hidebound themes. In 1958, digging on this site uncovered vestiges of a Palaeo-Christian edifice, raised to the memory of Saint Parteo, one of Corsica's comparatively unsung martyrs. It was unique in its conception in that it was constructed on a north-south axis, obviously the chapel of a very extensive cemetery.

Back now to Casamozzo, and eighteen kilometres down the road to Ponte Nuovo, from where with the aid of a map the student of military history can cover the whole of the fateful battleground and study the campaign's development, through the various acts to the final curtain.

The battle of Borgo with its echoes of the David and Goliath story made a deep impression in Europe. 'Gallant little Corsica' giving the big French bully a bloody nose, became the precursor of 'Gallant little Belgium' of 1914, and 'Gallant little Finland' of 1939. A little foresight, even so, should have made Corsican leaders realise that they could not continue to defy the might of France for any length of time. Unfortunately their surprising victory had gone to their heads, and a favourable opportunity of discussing reasonable terms lost through a false sense of invincibility.

For France, the defeat had been a severe shock. The King was furious. De Chauvelin was recalled in disgrace and his place taken by an experienced soldier, the Comte de Vaux, who arrived to assume command on 11 March 1769, bringing with him a further fourteen battalions to swell the French forces on the island to the unprecedented strength of 50,000. The Count made it quite clear that he was in deadly earnest. The day after landing he delivered an address to senior officers containing a stinging reproach for the purely defensive role they had adopted since Borgo.

The Corsicans, for their part, soon learnt that the future campaign would be no kid glove affair. In Calvi, a church was shelled by a mortar when packed for a religious festival. When part of the roof collapsed a large number of the congregation perished; those who fled from the ruins were hunted down. A small group of children hid in a tree. They were spotted by a sapper, Tourmagne, who 'loaded his wide-mouthed blunderbuss with a handful of shot, and going up to the tree blasted the wretched children from the branches as if they had been so many game birds'. On 3 May de Vaux issued an order of the day 'Do not spare the crops, vines, or olives of those who refuse to submit; terror is the only method by which they can be compelled to obey.'

This was the prelude to a general offensive launched by three columns under General d'Arcambal, the Comte de Vaux himself, and General de Marbeuf on the line Saint Florent-Oletta-Biguglia. Each column numbered roughly 12,000 men, and, of supreme importance, was supported by a powerful artillery group armed with the new Gribeauval canon, the most modern in any army, with a rate of fire of four rounds a minute and a range of 1200 metres. Against such a host, Pasquale Paoli could muster only 12,000 ill-armed militia with a few cannon, captured from the French and Genoese in previous campaigns.

Paoli's handling of this desperate situation was generally speaking as inept as that of Borgo had been brilliant. His original plan was to hold the cols on the line San-Pietro-di-Tenda-Murato-Borgo. It was too long a front, and in addition the devastating power of the Gribeauval cannon came as a total surprise. On 5 May, he gave the order for a general withdrawal to the Golo river, after d'Arcambal had stormed San-Pietro-di-Tenda, and the Comte de Vaux having driven the Patriots from Murato had seized the cols of Lento and Bigorno. It was at this point that Paoli committed a fatal error.

In the days before sophisticated bridging equipment, the Golo river though not particularly wide, running as it does between steep banks, its current so strong that even a powerful swimmer would find it difficult to negotiate, was a formidable obstacle. The only bridge was at Ponte Nuovo. His obvious move was to withdraw his forces as quickly as possible to the right bank, and then blow up the bridge. His left protected by the Asco massif, his front by the river, his right by the sea, French logistic and numerical superiority would have been largely offset. Instead he made the disastrous, and incomprehensible, decision to try to fight with the river at his back. Setting up his Headquarters at Rostino, he gave orders for his commanders to hold their new positions on the left bank, and for two companies of Prussian mercenaries – his only foreign troops – under Gentile, to fortify the bridge itself, hold it to the last, and deny the crossing of it to *all and everyone*.

On 7 May de Vaux stormed the two vital outposts of Lento village and Canavaggia. This reverse should have brought Paoli to his senses. He could still have re-grouped the bulk of his force on the right bank. Instead he ordered Grimaldi, commanding a battalion some 2000 strong to counter-attack, and to make matters worse, Grimaldi, a brave but unskilled leader, himself made three fatal mistakes. He made no attempt to protect his flanks, he attacked at two o'clock in the afternoon instead of waiting till nightfall to exploit his knowledge and his enemy's ignorance of the terrain, and once the attack was launched made no provision for an ordered withdrawal.

Before the first onrush the French fell back, whereupon

other brave, enthusiastic, but undisciplined Patriots, left their
positions to join in what they thought was a second Borgo. By
so doing they fell into a Balaclava-like trap. The French
artillery was brought into position on the flanks, opening fire
with deadly accuracy at the same time as de Marbeuf's
column, moving in from the east, arrived on the scene. Too
late the order was given to cross the Golo.

Now, it seemed, Fate had turned her back on the cause of
independent Corsica, and the tide of battle plumbed the
depths of pure tragedy. Obeying their instructions to the
letter, the Prussians holding the bridge had raised a small
protective wall to bar the entrance, and at the sight of a mass
of men obviously making for the bridge with intent to cross to
the opposite bank, promptly opened fire from behind their *ad
hoc* fortification. It was a massacre. Caught between two fires,
some ran for the Golo and plunged in only to be swept away
by the current, the turgid waters swollen by melted snow.
Others actually made a rampart of the bodies of their fallen
comrades and fought it out to the last. One group smashed a
way through to the bridge, to engage in a furious
hand-to-hand struggle with the leading French sections
following up, perishing at the point of the long French
bayonets. The defeat was total; irreparable.

The humpbacked Genoese bridge with its monument
commemorating the battle still stands, but I find it difficult to
believe that the dark patches on the stones are indeed, as
many claim, bloodstains that have been there ever since 9
May 1769.

Having visited the grave of Corsican nationalism, one
should now go to the birthplace of the man who came so near
to making the nationalist dream a permanent reality:
Morosaglia. This small town of 1222 inhabitants is set in the
green heart of the Castigniccia, the region which is mostly one
great chestnut forest. Like Bastelica, Sampiero's birthplace,
Morosaglia is actually a collection of hamlets, amongst them
Stretta, where Pasquale Paoli first saw the light of day in a
house fronting the N197 road from Ponte Leccia to San
Nicolau via Valle d'Alesani, which is now a museum. It is a

pleasant, intensely human, little museum, much in the same style as the Maison Mistral at Maillane, full of personal souvenirs, including amongst other things a collection of proclamations bearing the Moor's head crest, printed by the Press Paoli himself founded during the dizzily exciting days when Corsica belonged to the Corsicans*. On the walls are engravings of the portraits of the *Babbu della Patria,* one of the most popular subjects for portrait painters of the era. Gerard, Lawrence, and Drolling were amongst those anxious to persuade the romantic Corsican figure to sit for them.

Although originally buried in the church of Saint Pancras (London), his remains were brought back to the island on 3 September 1889, and now rest in a chapel, in what was the house's ground floor.

Morosaglia is also the resting place of Pasquale's elder brother Clemente, known as the 'Corsican Bayard', buried in the chapel of ancient Rostino convent where Paoli held a number of *Consultas,* now a school endowed in the terms of his will, while a short walk up hill is the old parish church of Santa Reparata where Pasquale was baptized. But even if one is not interested in history, this 'pilgrimage' is worth while if only because of the superb scenery – at its best from the Col de Prato four kilometres further on down the road – with its semi-circle of high peaks rising from the intense green of the meadows and the lush splendour of the chestnut groves; beyond, the sea and a dark shape rising on a clear day from the blue-green shimmer, the island of Elba.

Returning to the coastal road via Valle d'Alesani and Cervione, one should not be in too much of a hurry. Stop for a

* This emblem of the Moor's head – in fact more negroid than Moorish – dates from the time of Aragonese intervention in Corsica, when the Aragonese coat-of-arms included four Moors' heads, commemorating victories over the Saracens. Later, the island's only King, von Neuhoff, engraved his coinage with a single head. The idea appealed to Paoli who had it embroidered on the national flag as well as stamped on official documents. When Corsica became part of the Kingdom of France, the head figured beside the *fleur-de-lys,* while on becoming Baron Minto, Sir Gilbert Elliot had it incorporated in his personal coat-of-arms.

few minutes at the tiny village of Campana of only 80 inhabitants to look at the 'Adoration of the Shepherds' hung in the village church, which may well be the work of the Spanish painter Zurbaran or one of his pupils, and the church at Carcheto where the figures in the Stations of the Cross are dressed in the garb of Corsican peasants. That the idyllic setting can give a false impression of peace is proved by a story of a local vendetta of very recent times. In May 1912, François-Marie Castelli stabbed a girl for no other reason than that he suspected she had been giving food to one of his enemies. The wound was fatal, but the wretched girl did not die for eighteen hours. During this time not a soul dared to come to her aid for fear of reprisals, and when eventually she died, nobody dared make a coffin or in any way assist at her funeral, so that the *gendarmes* were obliged to bury her themselves.

Fourteen kilometres farther on is the commune of Valle d'Alesani in whose convent the charlatan von Neuhoff had himself crowned King Theodor I of Corsica, to embark on what must be one of the shortest reigns in history. Rather more interesting to art lovers is the picture by the Sienna master Sano di Pietro, 'The Virgin with the Cherry'. It was near Alesani, too, that the heretic sect the Giovannali were finally run to ground and exterminated on the orders of Pope Urban V.

At San Nicolau the road divides, and one should take the right fork, the D34, to return to the coastal road at Moriani Plage, a beach becoming increasingly popular with German holiday-makers. Continuing due south there is a fast, but dull stretch, eventually skirting the inland shores of the Etang de Diane, former mosquitoes' paradise, now exploited for its oyster beds and mussels, to reach the Tavignano river, with Aleria on the opposite bank.

A small island breaks the monotony of the lake's surface; the Ile des Pêcheurs, formed entirely of oyster shells, reminding us that oysters were a popular feature of Roman extravaganzas, and used to be sent salted from Aleria to the mainland. Always exposed to the danger of surprise attack from both land and sea, the city was built on a rise in the ground on the right bank which meant that in such flat country, it dominated the mouth of the river and the port. Prosper Mérimée was the first to insist that excavation of the site of the old settlement would be rewarding as long ago as 1840, but it was not till 1955 that serious work was undertaken.

The sixteenth-century Fort de Matra, houses the museum, Jérome Carcopino, with its collection of objects unearthed during the digging, but which I think is the more satisfactorily visited after, rather than before, walking round the actual excavations.

One enters from the north, looking straight down on the Forum, and to the left (east) the traces of what must have been an extremely wealthy home, known as the *Domus ad dolium,* so named because of the discovery of an enormous earthenware jar in one of the rooms at the far (north) end, probably part of the servants quarters. The Forum, 92 metres (100 yards) from east to west was colonnaded, lined with merchants' stalls, and entered under two arches from the west. To the west (right) is the Praetorium. The entrance arch, one column of which has been restored, gave onto the main building, the seat of government, each wall measuring some fifty metres, with a vast central patio and enclosing a *nympheum.* North of the Praetorium were the baths, essential feature of any Roman city. West of the *balneum* can be seen a recent discovery, the foundations of a building thought to have been a factory for conserving fish.

The museum, named after the archaeologist and historian of ancient Rome, Jérome Carcopino (1881-1970) is divided into eleven halls opening off the central patio of the Matra Fort. Halls 1 to 5 are devoted each to a specific era of the city's history, numbers three and four to the pre-Roman period, one of the showpieces (in number four) being a '*coupe Attique érotique!*, an explicitly amorous incident, work of the Greek Panaitos in the year 480 BC. The first hall – '*Vie economique et religieuse sous l'Empire Romain*' – contains show cases of gold and silver coins, pottery from early Christian Rome, household objects and work tools. The remaining halls, somewhat smaller are taken up with collections from tombs, including flagons and drinking vessels with complicated designs – Bacchus watching benevolently over the *vendange;* Hercules and the lion – my favourite, a scene depicting hell – jewellery, and helmets. New finds are continually coming to light and it is expected that the museum will be considerably enlarged.

Ghisonaccia, fourteen kilometres south of Aleria, capital of the eastern plain, is built by the mouth of the Fium Orbo (the blind) river. Till the mosquito had been defeated, Ghisonaccia, today a prosperous little town of 1500 inhabitants, had been described as a 'broken-down one-street village', accorded the suffix *'accia'* or *'acciu'* denoting 'bad', even 'accursed', in order to differentiate it from Ghisoni, a charming mountain village twenty-seven kilometres inland.

The road linking Ghisonaccia with Ghisoni, is another of these fabulous routes, part of the Corsican heritage, plunging through narrow gorges,the Inzecca and Strette,formed by the Fium Orbo cutting like a knife through great rocks and 'steep rugged mountains covered with sweet-scented shrubs' sometimes so narrow, so embedded that sunlight sarcely penetrates. One writer, in fact, stated that he had 'the impression of being at the bottom of a coffin'.

Ghisoni itself, though 2000 feet above sea level, rather than the usual *village perché* is tucked away at the head of the valley, hemmed in by trees, and completely overshadowed by two mountains with the curious names of *Kyrie Elaison* and *Christe Elaison.* The names date from the time of the suppression of the Giovannali when several of the sect had been captured and were being burnt at the stake at the foot of these peaks. Although any form of religious comfort for the victims was strictly proscribed on the Bishop's orders, one old priest began to intone the service for the dead. At the first notes of the *Kyrie,* a dove began to circle above the stake, accepted by the dying men as a sign of salvation. On a less elevated level, Ghisoni was much appreciated by the older generation of British tourist as an excellent place for a few days fishing.

Always a turbulent region, the Fium Orbo was the last to

submit to French rule, and was scourged by the vendetta. Representatives of law and order were ignored, as were those of the church. One parish priest, however, made his mark, and his memory is still revered. At the first Mass celebrated, he startled the very toughest of his flock. 'Here is the Father' he said, taking a rifle from under the altar cloth and holding it over his head. 'Here is the Son' he continued, drawing a pistol from the folds of his surplice. 'And here is the Holy Ghost' he added, taking a Genoese dagger from its scabbard 'and I hope God gives you the good sense to see what I'm driving at.' He became so popular in this generally considered impossible parish, that he spent the rest of his active life with his tamed flock.

Another eighteen kilometres bring one to Solenzara and the end of the eastern plain. Like Bastia, at the northern extremity, Solenzara is the image of the Corsica of tomorrow, under the impulse of the sun-seeking tourist, concentrating on the *plages,* turning its back on forest and mountain, on meadow and torrent. Prosperity here is to be found in the development of the *Port de Plaisance,* in all forms of aquatic sport; deep-sea fishing, water-skiing, skin-diving; To refind the Corsica of Sampiero, Vincentello and Paoli, one must continue on to the the Sartenais and to Bonifacio, to that south still brooding over a sad yet nostalgic past.

12   The Sartenais

BONIFACIO

The Port of the Laestrygonians

'We entered this port well known to sailors closed in by sheer cliffs with two headlands converging to leave only a narrow passage for my ships which then proceeded to anchor side by side . . . I then organized a party to go on shore to find out to what bread-eaters the land belonged. On approaching the habitations, they saw a giantess drawing water from the source of the Bear, a limpid fountain; she was the daughter of Antiphates the Laestrygon. The men hailed her; they spoke to each other; they asked the name of the King, of his subjects: immediately she pointed out the towering roof of the paternal home.

But hardly had they entered the building indicated than they met the wife, large as a mountain, the sight of her striking them dumb. And she hastened to call her husband, King Antiphates from the *Agora,* who in turn had but one thought; to kill them without mercy. He crushed one of my men on whom he made a meal. The other two (of the landing party) fled back to the ships, but the alarm was given. Thousands of Laestrygonians came running and began to hurl down great blocks of rock from the cliffs: dying crews, shattered decks, a tumult of death rose from our ships. Then, having harpooned my men as if they were tuna fish, the giants carried them off for a fearful feast.'

This horrific story from the *Odyssey,* is generally agreed to be the first mention known of Bonifacio, for Ulysses's description tallies absolutely with the site of the old town. One might say that it is a fitting start to a story dominated largely by violence, war, and brutality, but relieved, nevertheless, by moments of sublime courage.

Once the Genoese had seized the town by guile in 1187, converting it into a fortress, siege after siege was withstood, and even more than Calvi, Bonifacio was to prove a thorn in the flesh of successive Corsican Patriot leaders. Much as the defence of Calvi has been praised, as a feat of arms it could hardly be compared with that of Bonifacio, lasting from 13 August 1420, till 5 January 1421.

The city owes its name to a certain Count Bonifacio of Lucca, ordered by Louis the Debonair to clear the island of the Saracens. At the head of a mixed force of Tuscans and locally recruited Corsicans, he was completely successful, following up his victories by leading an expedition against the Saracen stronghold of Carthage in August AD 828. Returning to the island, he then ordered a fortress to be built on the extreme southern tip which, after him, was to be named Bonifacio.

It was the Genoese, however, who brought the city its true aura of fame. In the thirteenth-century wars which opposed Genoa to the Pisans and the Patriots of Giudice di Cinarca, Bonifacio was the only place which remained firmly in Genoese hands. Pisa, as has been seen, was conclusively defeated at the battle of Meloria in 1284, and never again able to contest the rival Republic's hegemony, but in 1296, the cession of the island to Jaime I, King of Aragon, by the Pope Boniface VII, brought a new element to the scene. The Aragonese, however, seemed in no great hurry to take over their new possession. Half-hearted attempts to land in 1330 and again in 1335 were defeated. In the meantime Genoese power was on the increase. In defiance of the Pope Corsica was incorporated in the Republic, the first Governor arriving in 1359. These steps led to an alliance between the Corsicans and Aragon, whose joint forces inflicted a long series of defeats on the Genoese till by 1420, the whole island, with the exception of Bonifacio, was in their hands.

In the summer of that year, Alfonso V of Aragon, in the course of a ceremony held at Calvi, officially added Corsica to his Kingdom of Aragon, Catalonia, Sicily and Sardinia, appointing the Corsican hero, Vincentello d'Istria as Viceroy of the island.

It did not seem possible that the inhabitants of Bonifacio would even contemplate defying such a powerful combination as was now ranged against them, and there is no doubt that when Alfonso moved south with an army of veteran Spanish and Corsican troops commanded by Vincentello, and an armada of some eighty vessels, he was not expecting more than a token resistance.

By 12 August, the city had been invested from the land side, while the Spanish fleet after sailing up the narrow waters, had sunk every craft in the harbour and destroyed the vast reserves of wheat and wine stored on the quays. As if this were not enough to daunt the defenders, many Spanish units were armed with the most modern weapons in the world; a primitive form of cannon, known as the bombard, and muskets, whereas the Genoese did not possess a single firearm of any sort or description.

On 13 August, the first assault was launched after calls to surrender had been contemptuously ignored. To the anger and amazement of both Alfonso and Vincentello, it was decisively repulsed, the attackers suffering heavy losses. The bombards had done superficial damage to the battlements and caused a number of casualties, but the massive walls had withstood the solid shot well, and as the first assault waves came swarming up the scaling ladders, they were met not only by a hail of arrows, but also with cascades of boiling oil and burning sulphur.

The people of Bonifacio were indeed fighting for an ideal; their collective land and individual liberty. Within the framework of the Most Serene Republic, they enjoyed a privileged position. To encourage settlement in such a barren, unfriendly, but strategically important region, Genoa had not only allowed the city to assume the status of a republic within the Republic, but also paid each family a yearly subsistence allowance. Ruled by an elected *Podesta* (Mayor) aided by a council of four *anziani* and a legislative assembly of sixty members, Bonifacio was totally autonomous, and though under the protection of the mother city, not subject to any taxes save those imposed locally. The determination to preserve this freedom, not to fall under Aragon's notoriously harsh yoke, inspired the defence from the very beginning, banishing all thought of capitulation. It was not only the tough, well-trained city militia who lined the ramparts. Every able-bodied citizen – old men, priests, women, young girls, children – was under arms, and annals of the siege mention particularly the combative qualities of the married women, outstanding among them a certain Margarita Bobbia, always to be found where the action was the hottest, battling like a tigress with any weapon on which she could lay her hands.

Renewed attacks met with no more success than the first, and a scheme to create a gap in the defence by a shock force protected within a hollow tower on wheels, which could be manhandled up to the walls, was frustrated when a small band of Bonifacians made a daring night sortie, burning the machine as it was on the point of completion. By mid-September, alarmed by steadily mounting casualties, Alfonso decided to abandon attempts to storm the city, and instead, by ensuring that no one and nothing either entered or left from the gates, starve the obstinate inhabitants into submission. Though slow, these tactics proved effective. By December, as the siege was about to enter into its fifth month, lack of food was so acute that 'everything that could possibly contribute to human sustenance was eaten, cats, rats and weeds, and the pious wives of Bonifacio freely gave of their milk to relations, brothers, children, connexions (*sic*) and godfathers.'

The situation was desperate, especially as Alfonso, convinced that starvation must be taking its toll, was again hurling his men at the ramparts. Yet the Bonifacians refused to give up hope. They could not believe that Genoa would abandon them to their fate. It could only be a question of days, the *Podesta* felt, before a relief force hove in sight, and in an endeavour to gain time, sent an envoy to the enemy camp to discuss surrender terms. Alfonso, a volatile young man only twenty-six years of age, by now thoroughly bored by the whole affair, jumped at the chance of speedy negotiation and thereby fell into a trap, agreeing to suspend hostilities in return for twenty-seven hostages and the promise of unconditional surrender if, after forty days, no reinforcements were forthcoming.

The Genoese were fully aware of Bonifacio's plight, but the Doge had other more pressing affairs to occupy his mind, and the despatch of a relief force was delayed. When at last it did sail, contrary winds drove it off course so that by the time the forty days had run out, no welcome sail had appeared over the eastern horizon. At this critical moment, the defenders lived up to their reputation of being as cunning as they were courageous. When Alfonso sent a deputation to demand the keys of the city, the *Podesta* stated that he refused to comply with the demand for the simple reason that the awaited reinforcements had indeed arrived. Next morning, the bewildered Spaniards and Corsicans saw the ramparts swarming with men in armour, the sun glinting on the spears. They did not – could not – guess that most of these men were in fact women of Bonifacio dressed in the armour of fallen militia. Fighting was resumed, the weakened garrison still miraculously holding on, till, on Christmas Day, the longed for sails were sighted.

It is said that to begin with the vast Spanish fleet seemed so formidable that the Genoese commander, Giovanni Fregoso, hesitated to attack, but was persuaded to do so by Margarita Bobbia's husband, Angelo, who had swum out to pilot the rescuers through the narrow channel. Other strong swimmers diving from the cliff tops, cut the moorings of a number of the Spanish vessels, and in the ensuing confusion, the numerically inferior Genoese fleet scored a notable victory.

Massive supplies were unloaded. But recovering from their surprise, the dispersed Spanish force was able to concentrate and blockade the entrance to the narrows. For five anxious days it looked as though Fregoso's flotilla might be trapped till, following on the course of two fire ships, the Genoese were able to break through the ring and gain the open sea.

Despite this success Bonifacio's ordeal was by no means over, indeed the city might well have fallen had relentless pressure on the defences been maintained. Alfonso, however, profoundly discouraged, had now lost all interest. To his delight he received a message from Queen Jeanne of Naples, at war with both France and Genoa, offering to make him her heir in return for his armed intervention. The next day, 5 January, 1421, taking the twenty-seven hostages with him, he sailed for Naples, leaving his disconsolate Viceroy to his own devices.

Vincentello had no alternative but to raise the siege. Though he remained Viceroy for another fourteen years, he made no attempt to avenge this humiliating reverse.

At the very first sight of Bonifacio on its glaring white limestone plinth, one can well understand that, occupied by a determined garrison, the city deserves that much abused qualification of 'impregnable'. Of all the fortress towns of this island which specialises in such military architecture, it is the most inspired, for the *Haute Ville* is built on the very edge of cliffs, not merely sheer, but in many cases overhanging. In fact I should be most unwilling to inhabit one of the outer houses in case a tremor, or simply erosion, provoked a collapse of the rock structure, and cliff and houses together hurtled into the sea.

The citadel, culminating point of the *Haute Ville*, as in Calvi and Corte is now a Foreign Legion barracks. Outside the arched entrance stands a memorial to Legionaires who fell in the Sud-Oranais campaign of 1897-1902, a campaign which included an epic march of 1250 miles across the Sahara at the height of summer and the savage battle of El Moungar. Like the famous monument, *La Légion A Ses Morts,* unveiled in 1933 on the occasion of the Legion centenary, and now in Aubagne, this memorial was brought over from Algeria in 1962; further proof of the fact that the Legion never abandons its dead!

The barracks, of course, cannot be visited except on invitation, but the fine old church of Saint Dominic is open to the public. Generally believed to have been built by the Templars at the beginning of the fourteenth century, though there are theories that, on the contrary, it is the work of the Dominicans, it is the only Gothic edifice on the island. The interior, however, is Genoese baroque and contains two remarkable groups of painted wood, the one representing the Martyrdom of Saint Barthélemy – the unfortunate man was flayed alive – the other, the Three Marys at the foot of the Cross.

The sculptors certainly were gifted with a vivid imagination, combined with a highly developed sense of the dramatic.

The first group is an enormous work which it is proudly claimed 'weighs *800 kilos*', and together with a statue of the Virgin draped in black, is carried in procession on Good Friday. It shows the Saint bound to a stake, pouring with blood, while two tormentors, dressed after the fashion of Verdian Otellos, and carrying what look like butchers' knives, close in to carry on with their work. Supreme touch of horror is contributed by the figure of a mangy pariah dog straining to get at the freshly peeled flesh. In more spiritual mood, the features of the Three Marys are impregnated with grief. One understands that for them, as yet, there has been no revelation of the Resurrection, that the world is a world of sorrow. Both groups could be branded 'theatrical', but nevertheless both are moving.

The old town is really every bit as much a fortress as the designated citadel. Here again one finds the urban architecture of a city living in constant fear of aggression; narrow streets, many of them spanned by arches, houses of four or five storeys, walls sheer and smooth presenting no possible grip or foothold for a potential attacker, windows of almost loophole proportion. The steps leading up to high-set front doors are a modern addition. Originally one had to enter or leave one's home by means of a step ladder which was drawn up immediately after use; even the interior staircases, steep and narrow, were designed as a further obstacle to anyone who might have broken in onto the ground floor. Describing the staircase in the house in which he lodged, Lear writes 'it was such as a climbing South American monkey might have rejoiced in'.

The parish church of Sainte-Marie Majeure, where the Bonifacians prayed so fervently for the appearance of Giovanni Fregoso's ships, is in this part of the city. A twelfth-century construction, it is choked by the crush of surrounding houses, and from the outside is most noticeable for a sort of loggia masking the facade, where the notaries used to meet to draw up acts and discuss the legal problems of the day. One finds the church mentioned no less than 200 times in the archives of the thirteenth century.

The 'Treasure', guarded in the sacristy includes a very precious relic, a morsel of the True Cross, given as an ex-voto by Saint Helena, mother of Constantine, after narrowly escaping being shipwrecked in the course of a violent storm sweeping the notoriously treacherous Bonifacian Straits. Since then, this relic has been kept in a cupboard needing two keys, one retained by the *Podesta* the other by the Curé. When a particularly strong gale blew up, the *Podesta* and the *anziani* would go to the *Presbytère*, and from there with the Curé hurry to the church to collect the relic. The procession then moved on to the point known as *La Manichella* looking straight down on the water from a height of over 2000 feet, to bless and appease the angry sea. Other notable figures obliged to take refuge in Bonifacio harbour after narrow escapes from the fury of the Strait were Saint Francis of Assisi in 1215, and the great and all-powerful Emperor Charles V in 1541. The house where the latter was lodged, that of Count Cattaccioli, still stands, its door crowned by a marble lintel, and is just opposite that occupied by Napoleon from 22 January to 3 March 1793, when he was commanding the 2nd battalion of Corsican Volunteers, concentrating in Bonifacio prior to the unsuccessful Sardinian campaign.

There is no doubt that with the merger with France, Bonifacio lost much of its originality. Modern standardization has tended to iron out those sociological and ethnic differences between it and the rest of the island; but not entirely. The visitor frequently finds that even with a knowledge of French he cannot make himself understood. Away from the island, a Bonifacian is unlikely to greet you with that defiant pride *Je suis Corse*. He would more probably insist on his Genoese, Sardinian, or Neapolitan origin. Perhaps it would have been different if Napoleon had been a citizen of Bonifacio!

Though it could never be claimed that Bonifacio is a tourist centre after the pattern of Calvi or Bastia, the tourist trade has not entirely passed the city by. At the head of the inlet is – almost inevitably – a *port de plaisance* and the Marina, an agglomeration of houses fronting the quayside under the shadow of the citadel's cliffs. Of more recent construction, the Marina has a good, but not cheap, restaurant specializing in fish, and on the main street, the Quai Comparetti, two *boîtes de nuit*, but the chief attraction is the sea. There are no stretches of sandy *plage*. Bonifacio is not for those who simply wish to paddle and on returning home display a bronzed torso, but rather for the genuine swimmer, the deep-sea fisherman, and someone who enjoys sailing when the winds are strong.

A very 'different' sort of excursion is to the *grottes marines* (sea caves) *Le Camere, Le Bain de Venus,* and the *Sdragonato,* in the cliffs to the north just beyond the mouth of the inlet. By far the most spectacular is the *Sdragonato,* not unlike Capri's Blue Grotto. Once past the low stalactite hung entrance – which can be dangerous, or even impossible, to negotiate if the wind is blowing from the wrong direction – the water, greeny-blue and streaked with red and violet, takes on an extraordinary lucent quality, alternating with the deepest shadow accentuated at times by wafer-thin shafts of sunlight, for the roof – or ceiling – of the cave has a long, straight, narrow opening, above which can be seen the blue of the sky. It is as though, in a temper, one of the Laestrygonian giants had seized a huge axe and split the earth at his feet. The décor is truly theatrical; Nature's theatre, outdoing the most imaginative setting for the underwater scene from *Sadko*.

From the *Sdragonato,* continue the excursion by cruising, or rowing, down the open sea side of the headland on which the *Haute Ville* is built. Only by so doing can one fully appreciate this amazing natural fortress where again Nature outdoes man, for not even the great Vauban himself could have improved on this site. Midway down the outer cliff, 187 rough steps have been carved in the face. They purport to be the single night's work of Alfonso's soldiers hoping thereby to surprise the garrison, but are in fact natural steps formed by fisherman who, ever since the city was founded, used the track in calm weather.

The men who make a living by ferrying tourists round the *grottes* and down this stretch of coast, have a standard joke. Pointing out the steps and stressing the fact that they were carved in the space of a *single* night, they add *'C'est pas chez nous en Corse que l'on ferait cela'* ('We Corsicans wouldn't do anything like that') – a caustic reference to the Corsican's unjustified reputation for idleness.

SARTENE

La plus corse des villes Corses

This observation by Prosper Merimée still holds good today, Sartène a sub-prefecture, a town of some 6000 inhabitants, is indeed the most introvert of Corsican cities, even more deeprootedly nationalist than Corte, for whereas the latter has evolved along the path of compromise with the second half of the twentieth century, Sartène clings fiercely to the past, and this despite the fact that it was founded by the Genoese in – for Corsica — the comparatively recent era of the sixteenth century.

After the defeat of Rinuccio della Rocca, the Genoese hoped to diminish the other threat to their authority in the south, that of the Saracens, by the construction of a powerful fortress in a favourable natural setting. The contrary happened. The Saracens saw the construction of Sartène as a challenge which they were prompt to answer. In 1538, an expedition led by the Bey of Algiers, landed on the southern shore of the Gulf of Valinco, stormed the city and, after a week's uninterrupted loot and pillage, returned to their African stronghold with 400 prisoners who were then sold as slaves.

It is not for its struggles against Moslem pirates or foreign invaders, however, that the city is best known, and has carved itself a name, but for the bitter hatred between its inhabitants, so great that for years it was the theatre of what could almost be described as a minitature Civil War. All Corsica, with the exception possibly of Cap Corse, abounds with tales of family vendettas, but in Sartène this was indeed the vendetta on a grand scale for it split the whole town into two factions, due largely to the local social pattern.

The Sartènais district is essentially an area of large properties, owned by a minor nobility calling themselves the *sgio* (abbreviation for *signori*), whose claims to nobility were recognized as a conciliatory gesture to the islanders by Louis XVI, even though many were sadly lacking in culture, some fifty indeed, it is said, unable to write their own names. Nevertheless the influence they wielded was considerable, so that when the principal families actually living in the city fell out – the Roccaserras, the Pietri and the Ortoli – the entire population was dragged into the quarrel which came to a head in 1830 when revolution overthrew the last of the Bourbons, Charles X, to replace him by Louis-Philippe. The Roccaserras who lived in the upper, Santa Anna, part of the town were the 'Whites' – supporters of Charles; while in the lower, Borgo, quarters, the Pietris and Ortolis, supporters of the new régime were looked upon as 'Reds'.

'War' opened when the Ortolis, in direct contravention to the Roccaserra Mayor's order and supported by the Pietris, formed a National Guard and began a triumphant march through the streets. Roccaserra's method of demonstrating his disapproval, was to order his supporters to open fire on the parade, the first volleys killing two men – one of them Sebastien Pietri – and wounding five. Next day supporters of both sides moved in from the country, and for some days any movement in the streets drew down heavy fire which rapidly degenerated into a general ragged battle with neither faction able to claim the advantage.

The official powers of law and order were helpless. No convictions were forthcoming, in spite of such flagrant breaches of the peace, the general situation still further complicated by the fact that the initial disorders were the fault of the party supporting the new government. The roused passions quieted, but did not die, and three years later, in a lonely corner of the Rizzanese river valley, Roccaserras and Pietris again met head-on. Sebastien Pietri's two brothers, Camille and Alexandre were killed while Jerome Roccaserra, brother of the Mayor who had given the order to fire on the National Guard, sustained a grave wound in the arm, from which, however, he recovered. The Roccaserras followed up this success by ambushing a group of Pietris two months later, again killing two of their rivals.

At this stage the French authorities stepped in, in the form of the island's Military Governor, Baron Lallemand, a Napoleonic general and one of the peers of the Empire, a born adventurer, a man temperamentally in sympathy with such unruly subjects as the Corsicans, and their idealistic passions for lost causes. He himself had emigrated to the United States after the Hundred Days, where he had tried to organize a sea-borne expedition to rescue the fallen Emperor from Saint Helena. Louis XVIII thought him likely to be a trouble-maker and banned him from France, but Louis-Philippe rehabilitated him, and then, possibly to keep him from further scheming, appointed him Corsica's military Governor, a position he fulfilled so successfully to the mutual satisfaction both of Paris and the islanders, that he was maintained in office till his death in 1839.

The 'Peace of Sartène' a colourful, dramatic event, was Lallemand's brain-child. In December 1834, after lengthy talks, the leaders of the warring families attended Mass together, then swore on the high altar to eschew further acts of violence, after which, adjourning to the vestry, they signed the official peace document. One of the signatories was a priest, uncle of the three dead Pietri brothers whom he had loved as if they had been his own sons, and who, because of his calling unable to take the law into his own hands, had, as a sign of mourning, shut himself up in his house, blocked all the windows so that he lived in permanent darkness, and thrown away his razor. He signed out of a sense of duty as a priest, but this did not alter his way of life or prevent him from hoping that some day the vengeance which he could not undertake would be exacted.

The peace was kept largely due to Lallemand's influence, but it was an uneasy peace. The atmosphere remained explosive. People would not walk the streets other than in small groups, and armed. Windows remained reduced to the size of loopholes for fear of snipers.

Curiously enough it was not a sudden flare of irrepressible passion which led to a renewal of the shooting, but a passage in Merimée's best-selling novel, *Colomba,* which was based on the history of a vendetta in nearby Fozzano village, but in which a number of individual incidents were drawn from the author's general knowledge of the island's blood feuds.

In the climax, Merimée had described how his hero, though badly wounded in the arm, had nevertheless managed to kill his two enemies. It was actually based on the story of the clash between Jerome Roccaserra and Alexandre and Camille Pietri. All would have been well had not Merimée, afraid of being accused of gross exaggeration added a footnote to the effect that anyone who doubted the possibility of such a feat, could go to Sartène, and there learn the facts pertaining to a certain incident.

Still sealed hermit-like in his house, the Abbé Pietri obtained a copy of the book. It heaped coals of fire on his head. Not only had Jerome Roccaserra, now living a comfortable bourgeois life, killed his beloved nephews, he had infringed the whole gamut of honour's unwritten code by boasting of the fact – and to a stranger. Unwillingly Merimée, who had enjoyed Jerome's hospitality, describing him as one of Sartène's 'most distinguished and agreeable citizens', had signed his host's death warrant. In 1843, nine years after his killing of Alexandre and Camille, Jerome was in turn ambushed and killed on the Propriano road. It was common knowledge that the assassins had been paid by the Abbé, who celebrated Jerome's funeral by shaving his beard and opening up his rooms to the light of day.

Sartène is a lonely town, surprisingly isolated for an island where lack of space makes habitations tend to bunch like sheep. But here, without detailed knowledge of the map, a stranger might feel he was approaching an islet of Asia's land-ocean. This first view of Sartène has reminded some not so much of a medieval European citadel, but rather of Lhassa, an illusion due most probably to the rising barrier formed by each row of houses towering to seven, even eight storeys. This illusion is admirably caught by Lear, with his highly developed sense of the vertical. I prefer 'Sartène' to any other of his Corsican paintings, seizing as it does not only the soaring quality, but also the brooding remoteness.

Once within the city, the sombre atmosphere is contagious. The people of Sartène are certainly not ebullient. There is nothing of the Italian sparkle here. It is many years since the last of the 'great' bandits, Muzarettu, died of cancer in a Franciscan monastery, in officially recognized sanctuary, but there is a lurking feeling that, at any moment, some minor incident might spark off a tale of violent death. This impression is somehow heightened by the very construction of the houses. Those of Bonifacio could be qualified as flimsy in comparison with those of Sartène. Huge blocks of stone are used, not only in the foundations, but in the walls. From each solid plinth the walls slope slightly inwards, after the manner of the High Atlas Kasbahs, which even a Barbary ape might find difficulty in scaling. Most of the streets could more happily be described as alleys, darkened by vaults and arches so that at times progress is almost groping.

Every facet bears the stamp of a habitation designed primarily for defence; the solid down-to-earth Town Hall, for a time occupied by the local Genoese Governor, the facade of the parish church. The men gathered round outside tables of the main square's cafés would, one fancies, really be more at ease inside, protected by stone or bricks and mortar. Do not expect even the sober animation of the Bonifacio Marina. When Calvi and Bastia are as sky-scraper ridden, juke-box deafened, package-tour invaded as the Costa Brava, Sartène is likely to remain a little corner of Tibet in the Mediterranean.

It is fitting that the aloof Sartènais should be the region in which recently the most astonishing archaeological finds have come, and are still coming, to light. If the east coast plain is the keep of classical Corsica, the territory to the south of the Taravo river is the treasure-store of an era of such antiquity as to make the days of Greece and Rome appear contemporary, taking us back to the fifth and sixth millenium BC.

In the mid-nineteenth century when Merimée was touring the island, a few menhirs and dolmens were to be found lying forlornly on uncultivated land, arousing little or no interest. Even in the twenties one reads 'of prehistoric relics in the way of buildings, tombs and other remains of man's handiwork, there is practically nothing'. The picture has changed radically since the war, thanks chiefly to the efforts of the archaeologist Roger Grosjean responsible for the beginning of properly organized research in this field in 1954. Today it seems proven that 'about 3500 years ago, for the first time in Europe, artists in Corsica created and fashioned large statues in the image of man at a time when art was still in the stage of symbolism . . . certain of these works preceded classical statuary by centuries.' It would also seem certain that this basically artistic race was conquered and eventually destroyed by a more warlike people to whom Grosjean has given the name Torreens because of their habit of raising stone, tower-like buildings. One might say indeed that Corsica's story was a rehearsal for that of Greece and Rome.

The most important discoveries have been made in the neighbourhood of the hamlet of Filitosa, eighteen kilometres from the west coast resort of Propriano, and within two kilometres of the village of Sollarcaro, ancient home of the great d'Istria family. The hamlet has now become the *Station Prehistorique de Filitosa,* and the farmer beneath whose lands so many of these treasures had lain hidden for the best part of 5000 years, Monsieur Césari, is now designated *Propriétaire-Conservateur.* The discoveries have materially altered his way of life. Probably more people have visited

Filitosa in the last decade than in the preceding thousand years, and the number increases as the ancient Torreen *oppidum*, on the spur of land overlooking the confluence of the little Barcajolo and Sardelle rivers is still further developed, becoming a visual précis of the dawn of human history, rather than pre-history.

The *oppidum* is 130 metres long by 40 metres wide and contains three main buildings known as the *Monuments Est, Central*, and *Ouest*. Crossing the Sardelle, the *route d'accès* enters the *oppidum* by the *Monument Est*. It is a purely Torreen construction, but the Torreens who one now realises had highly developed iconoclastic tendencies, used morsels of the work of their more artistic predecessors, classified here as 'Megalithics', in their buildings. This can be seen in the *Monument Central*, thought to have been a form of temple, where considerable fragments of megalithic statue-menhirs have been incorporated in the walls, and outside where a statue-menhir, somewhat prosaically known as Filitosa IX, has been set up as ocular proof of Monsieur Grosjean's theory. Certainly there is nothing symbolic about this. People like to compare the statue-menhirs with some of the work of the late Pablo Picasso, but though the outlines are of an extreme symplicity, there is nothing impressionist, fauvist, cubist, about the features. Despite eyeless sockets, lipless mouths, there is a fundamental naturalism, an evocation of life prefiguring a Winged Victory rather than a section of 'Guernica'.

Filitosa, it is also thought was the field of the last great battle fought between Torreens and 'Megalithics', witnessing the final defeat of the latter, the *Monument Ouest* at the point of the rocky spur overlooking the rivers' confluence, originally the memorial to celebrate this triumph. Across the Barcajolo, in a field dotted with olive trees, a little semi-circle of five statue-menhirs has been set up. As three of them are armed figures, they make an impressive eternal and unchanging Guard of Honour to their own past.

To end this journey on which I have tried not merely to discover the physiognomy, but something of the spirit of

Corsica, one cannot do better than return to Sartène for Holy Week, and the Good Friday procession of the *Catenacciu.*

The length and breadth of the Northern Mediterranean shores, from Salonika to Sevilla, it is not the comfortable, homely festival of Christmas, but the drama of Easter, which is the dominant event of the Christian year. Physically and emotionally during the six weeks of Lent building up to the climax of the twelve strokes of midnight to greet the risen Christ with an explosion of joy, for many the tragedy of Good Friday becomes not merely a date in the church calendar, but a day of personal mourning; and nowhere in the Western Mediterranean is this drama so deeply felt as in Sartène,

The traditional *Catenacciu,* meaning the 'chained one', is a re-enaction of the original Calvary, the like of which could be seen only at Oberammagau. Christ, barefooted, robed in scarlet, his face hidden by a hood, not pointed like those worn in Sevilla's *semana santa,* but crushed onto the skull, drags an enormous black cross, normally kept in the Parish church, only brought out for this special occasion, while a heavy chain, clamped round his right ankle, sets up a mournful clanking as it is jerked over the cobbles. Mystery surrounds this figure referred to as the *Grand Penitent.* He is a volunteer for this exhausting, harrowing role, his identity known only to the priest who at his request has confided it to him. It is generally accepted that he is a criminal acting in a spirit of genuine repentance, hoping to obtain a degree of salvation by mortification of the flesh, but his secret must be inviolate, and Geoffrey Wagner says that 'only a year or so ago, a Christ whose anonymity was being threatened by an onlooker, produced a pistol from under his cloak'.

Close on the heels of the *Grand Penitent,* a figure dressed in white, representing Simon of Cyrene, endeavours to help bear the great weight of the cross. He is followed by priests, choir, some chosen parishioners and finally a group of eight *Black Penitents,* four of them carrying a bier on which is laid a figure of Christ brought down from the cross, hands and feet bloodied, a gash in his side, the body sprinkled with petals, the other four holding up a black palanquin.

Up through the streets and alleys, the procession follows its long path between a human hedge, windows candle-lit, jammed by the old and very young children, through the vault of the Town Hall, till it reaches its final destination, the main square. There the priest delivers a sermon, then blesses the crowd before it disperses, making the sign of the cross with the figure of the dead Christ taken from the bier.

For the *Grand Penitent* the evening is a genuine ordeal. The weight of the cross must be crushing. The chain cannot help his progress, and when he stumbles and falls three times as tradition demands, the falls may not always be simulated. Till comparatively recent years, the crowd often worked itself up into a frenzy. The *Penitent* would be belaboured with sticks, stoned, spat on. Today, however, that mass identification with the people of Jerusalem has become a thing of the past.

There are some – mostly smug Nordics, it must be admitted – who register disapproval at such a public display of raw emotion. Personally, I see such demonstrations as a mirror of the Corsican spirit, a spirit which kept alive the will to fight against impossible odds for over 1000 years of unremitting suffering and tribulation. Napoleon insisted that the word 'impossible' was not French; he should have said not 'Corsican'. While other European nations were enjoying the fruits of successive cultural expressions and social innovations, for Corsicans, the legacy of passing centuries remained the bitter, bloody struggle to preserve even a semblance of freedom. Yet no other nation of so small a population has seen so many of its sons take their place in the Gallery of the Great.

That hint of pride in the three words, *Je suis Corse,* is not misplaced.

Index